Shadow Education in the Middle East

This book offers insights into the role of private supplementary tutoring in the Middle East, and its far-reaching implications for social structures and mainstream education. Around the world, increasing numbers of children receive private tutoring to supplement their schooling. In much of the academic literature this is called shadow education because the content of tutoring commonly mimics that of schooling: as the curriculum changes in the schools, so it changes in the shadow.

While much research and policy attention has focused on private tutoring in East Asia and some other world regions, less attention has been given to the topic in the Middle East. Drawing on both Arabic-language and English-language literature, this study commences with the global picture before comparing patterns within and among 12 Arabic-speaking countries of the Middle East. It presents the educational and cultural commonalities amongst these countries, examines the drivers of demand and supply of shadow education, and considers the dynamics of tutoring and how it impacts on education in schools.

In addition to its pertinence within the Middle East itself, the book will be of considerable interest to academics and education policy makers broadly concerned with changing roles of the state and private sectors in education.

Mark Bray is Distinguished Chair Professor and Director of the Centre for International Research in Supplementary Tutoring (CIRIST) in the Faculty of Education at East China Normal University, Shanghai. He is also Emeritus Professor holding the UNESCO Chair in Comparative Education at the University of Hong Kong. He has written extensively on shadow education in many settings across the world.

Anas Hajar is Associate Professor of Multilingual Education, and the PhD Programme Director, in the Faculty of Education at Nazarbayev University, Kazakhstan. He is particularly interested in motivational issues in language learning and in intercultural engagement. He also works in the areas of shadow education, internationalisation, education abroad and language learning strategies.

Shadow Education in the Middle East

Private Supplementary Tutoring and its Policy Implications

Mark Bray and Anas Hajar

United Nations
Educational, Scientific and
Cultural Organization

UNESCO Chair in Comparative Education
• The University of Hong Kong

United Nations
Educational, Scientific and
Cultural Organization

LONDON AND NEW YORK

First published 2023
by Routledge
4 Park Square, Milton Park, Abingdon, Oxon OX14 4RN

and by Routledge
605 Third Avenue, New York, NY 10158

Routledge is an imprint of the Taylor & Francis Group, an informa business

in collaboration with the Centre for International Research in Supplementary Tutoring (CIRIST), East China Normal University (ECNU), Shanghai, the UNESCO Chair in Comparative Education at the University of Hong Kong (HKU), and the UNESCO Regional Center for Educational Planning (RCEP) in United Arab Emirates.

© 2023 Mark Bray and Anas Hajar

The right of Mark Bray and Anas Hajar to be identified as authors of this work has been asserted in accordance with sections 77 and 78 of the Copyright, Designs and Patents Act 1988.

The Open Access version of this book, available at www.taylorfrancis.com, has been made available under a Creative Commons Attribution-Non Commercial-No Derivatives 4.0 license. No part of this book may be reprinted or reproduced or utilised in any form or by any electronic, mechanical, or other means, now known or hereafter invented, including photocopying and recording, or in any information storage or retrieval system, without permission in writing from the publishers.

Trademark notice: Product or corporate names may be trademarks or registered trademarks, and are used only for identification and explanation without intent to infringe.

Disclaimer: The designations employed and the presentation of material throughout this publication do not imply the expression of any opinion whatsoever on the part of the publishers, CIRIST, ECNU, HKU, RCEP or UNESCO concerning the legal status of any country, territory, city or area or of its authorities, or the delimitation of its frontiers and boundaries.

The authors are responsible for the choice and the presentation of the facts in this book and for the opinions expressed therein, which are not necessarily those of the above-named bodies.

British Library Cataloguing-in-Publication Data
Names: Bray, Mark, 1952– author. | Hajar, Anas, 1985– author.
Title: Shadow education in the Middle East : private supplementary tutoring and
  its policy implications / Mark Bray and Anas Hajar.
Description: Abingdon, Oxon ; New York, NY : Routledge, 2023. | Includes bibliographical
  references and index.
Identifiers: LCCN 2022015234 (print) | LCCN 2022015235 (ebook) | ISBN 9781032329802
  (hardback) | ISBN 9781032329819 (paperback) | ISBN 9781003317593 (ebook)
Subjects: LCSH: Tutors and tutoring—Middle East. | Education—Middle East. |
  Education and state—Middle East.
Classification: LCC LC41 .B73 2023 (print) | LCC LC41 (ebook) | DDC
  371.39/40956—dc23/eng/20220606
LC record available at https://lccn.loc.gov/2022015234
LC ebook record available at https://lccn.loc.gov/2022015235

Library of Congress Cataloging-in-Publication Data
A catalog record for this book has been requested

ISBN: 978-1-032-32980-2 (hbk)
ISBN: 978-1-032-32981-9 (pbk)
ISBN: 978-1-003-31759-3 (ebk)

DOI: 10.4324/9781003317593

Typeset in Times New Roman
by Apex CoVantage, LLC

Contents

Acknowledgements vii
List of Abbreviations ix
List of Tables x
List of Figures xi
List of Boxes xii
Executive Summary xiii
Foreword xviii

1 **Introduction** 1

2 **Global perspectives on shadow education** 4
Definitions and scope 4
Providers and modes 5
Geographic and cultural variations 6
Positives and negatives 9

3 **Middle East contexts** 16
Educational and cultural commonalities 16
Social, economic and political diversities 17
Roles of the state 19

4 **Scale and nature of shadow education** 27
Enrolment rates 27
Modes and durations 33
Drivers of demand 36
Drivers of supply 42

5 Educational and social impact — 54
Learning gains 54
Backwash on schooling 57
Social values 58

6 Policy implications — 62
Designing and enforcing regulations 62
  Regulations concerning provision of private tutoring by serving teachers 62
  Regulations on tutorial centres 67
Making private tutoring less necessary 69
Engaging in partnerships 72

7 Conclusion — 83
Understanding the big picture 83
  Commonalities and diversities 83
  Roles of the state and of the market 86
Finding balances 88

Notes on the Authors — 98
Index — 100

Acknowledgements

Many organisations and individuals have contributed to this book. The authors cannot name them all, but can at least express appreciation to the most prominent.

First on the list is United Nations Educational, Scientific and Cultural Organization's (UNESCO's) Regional Center for Educational Planning (RCEP), led by its Director Mahra Hilal Almutaiwai. She gave not only overall guidance but also specific comments on a draft manuscript and links to individuals and institutions able to provide further information and analysis. Among her staff, our greatest appreciation is to Sahar ElAsad, who managed the work on the RCEP end with constant attention to detail, diplomacy and good humour, and brought her own very valuable substantive insights.

Core ingredients for the book included data from questionnaires distributed by RCEP and then inputs to a regional Policy Forum on 22 November 2021. The Policy Forum was attended by 33 participants, including personnel from Ministries of Education across the region, researchers with strong expertise in the theme, teachers and tutors. Many participants also drew on their own experiences as former students or as parents. The bilingual event in Arabic and English validated the core messages while also providing additional insights and access to follow-up material. Participants indicated that the event had also stimulated their own thinking about policy approaches and appropriate actions to address shadow education more effectively in their countries.

Also at the institutional level have been inputs and support from several universities. Foremost in this category are the Centre for International Research in Supplementary Tutoring (CIRIST) at East China Normal University (ECNU), of which Mark Bray is director, and Nazarbayev University in Kazakhstan of which Anas Hajar is a member of the professoriate. On a related plane, the work was conducted under the umbrella of the UNESCO Chair in Comparative Education at the University of Hong Kong, and is the latest geographic focus for work across many world regions conducted since establishment of the Chair in 2011.

Turning to further individuals, the authors thank the following for having commented on drafts and provided specific material: Nawfal Adnan, Aisha Alanzi, Thamir Aldaghishy, Mahmoud Dahroug, Munira Eskander, Jenaan Farhat, Sheren Hamed, Liu Junyan, Mohamed Alaa Abdel-Moneim, Valeria Rocha, Abdellatif Sellami, Ghassan Shughri, and Zhang Wei.

Abbreviations

ATA	Australian Tutoring Association
CIEFR	China Institute for Educational Finance Research
GCC	Gulf Cooperation Council
GDP	Gross Domestic Product
IB	International Baccalaureate
IIEP	International Institute for Educational Planning
IGCSE	International General Certificate of Secondary Education
ISIS	Islamic State of Iraq and Syria (also known as Islamic State of Iraq and the Levant – ISIL and by its Arabic acronym Daesh)
KHDA	Knowledge and Human Development Authority
MENA	Middle East and North Africa
OECD	Organisation for Economic Co-operation and Development
PISA	Programme for International Student Assessment
RCEP	Regional Center for Educational Planning
SACMEQ	Southern and Eastern Africa Consortium for Monitoring Educational Quality
SESRI	Social and Economic Survey Research Institute
SIM	Subscriber Identity Module
TIMSS	Trends in International Mathematics and Science Study
UNESCO	United Nations Educational, Scientific and Cultural Organization
UNICEF	United Nations Children's Fund
UNRWA	United Nations Relief and Works Agency

Tables

3.1	Features of Middle East Countries	17
3.2	National and Non-national Populations, GCC Countries	20
4.1	Scale of Shadow Education in Middle East Countries	28
4.2	Grade 8 Enrolment Rates and Motives in Supplementary Tutoring, TIMSS, 2015 and 2019 (%)	32
6.1	Regulations on Teachers Concerning Private Supplementary Tutoring in Middle East Countries	63
6.2	Regulations on Private Tutorial Centres in Middle East Countries	68

Figures

2.1	Diversity of Modes of Shadow Education Delivery	6
4.1	Enrolment Rates in Mathematics Supplementary Tutoring, Eight Countries, Grade 8, 2015 and 2019 (%)	33
4.2	Types of Private Tutoring, UAE, 2018	34
4.3	Durations of Mathematics Supplementary Tutoring, Eight Countries, Grade 8, 2019 (%)	34
4.4	Reasons for Securing Private Tutoring, by Gender, Qatar, 2018	40
4.5	Advertising of Tutoring Services, by Internet (Jordan) and Informal Wall Posters (Saudi Arabia)	44
5.1	The Tutor Who Can Do Everything?	56
5.2	Parental Perceptions of Change in Overall Academic Performance After Private Tutoring, UAE	57
6.1	Iraq Ministry of Education Circular on Private Tutoring, 2017	67

Boxes

2.1	Perceptions of Incidence – the Arab Region and Beyond	8
4.1	A Long-standing Issue	27
4.2	Harnessing Technology and Transcending National Boundaries	35
4.3	Parental Perspectives on Private Tutoring in Abu Dhabi	41
4.4	Teaching Deficiencies and Low Salaries Underpin Private Tutoring Even in a Rich Country	45
6.1	How Clearly Do Parents Know What They Are Getting?	74
7.1	A School-Driven Approach to Private Tutoring in Dubai	92

Executive summary

Around the world, increasing numbers of children receive private tutoring to supplement their schooling. In much of the academic literature, this is called shadow education because the content of tutoring to some extent mimics that of schooling: as the curriculum changes in the schools, so it changes in the shadow. The tutoring may be delivered one-to-one, in small groups, in large classes and over the internet. Some tutoring is provided by regular teachers in order to gain additional income, while other tutoring is provided through commercial enterprises. Informal suppliers including university students, retirees and casual workers form a third category in the delivery of tutoring.

While much research and policy attention has focused on shadow education in East Asia and some other world regions, less attention has been given to the topic in the Middle East. It deserves much more focus because of its far-reaching implications for social structures and for mainstream education systems. This study commences with the global picture before comparing patterns within and among 12 Arabic-speaking countries of the Middle East.

Definitions, scope and scale

The study is concerned with tutoring that is:

- *fee-charging*. The focus excludes fee-free tutoring by relatives or by teachers as part of their school duties.
- *academic*. The focus is on mathematics, languages and other examinable domains. It does not include musical, artistic, or sporting skills that are learned primarily for pleasure and/or more rounded personal development
- *supplementary*. The provision is additional to that provided by schools.

- for *primary and secondary* education. Shadow education in pre-primary and post-secondary education also deserves attention, but it is less voluminous and is excluded from this study to permit clear attention to the primary and secondary levels.

The 12 Middle East countries on which the study focuses can be considered in two groups. The six high-income countries of the Gulf Cooperation Council (GCC) comprise one group, and the six lower-income countries comprise the other group. The GCC members are Bahrain, Kuwait, Oman, Qatar, Saudi Arabia and the UAE; and the countries in the second group are Iraq, Jordan, Lebanon, Palestine, Syria and Yemen.

Of course, much diversity of economic and social characteristics exists within each group. For example, within the GCC group per capita gross domestic product (GDP) ranged from US$70,700 in Qatar to US$19,300 in Oman; and within the other group, it ranged from US$9,300 in Lebanon to US$900 in Yemen. Diversity was also evident in the proportions of non-nationals in the populations and in political structures. The diversity provides instructive variables for comparative analysis of private tutoring patterns.

Concerning the scale of tutoring, data from the Trends in International Mathematics and Science Study (TIMSS) provide some indication of enrolment rates combining fee-charging and fee-free supplementary tutoring. The following bar chart shows statistics for supplementary tutoring received by Grade 8 students for mathematics in 2019.

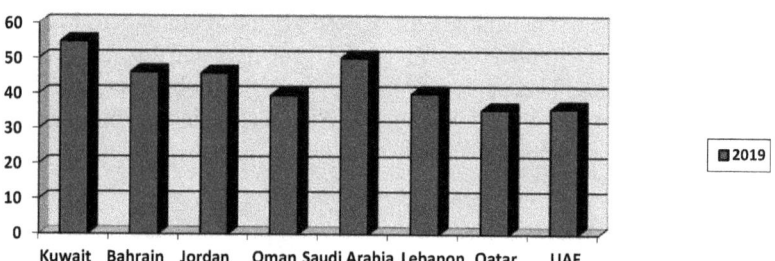

Enrolment Rates in Mathematics Supplementary Tutoring, Grade 8 (%).

Other snapshots of data include:

- *Iraq*: A 2019/20 random survey in four schools found that 71% of Grade 11 students were receiving private supplementary tutoring.
- *Kuwait*: A 1% random sample of parents throughout the country reported in 2012 indicated that 44% of children across all grades were receiving tutoring.

- *Qatar*: Data collected by the Social and Economic Survey Research Institute (SESRI) in 2018 indicated private tutoring enrolment rates of 38% in Grade 8 and 56% in Grade 12.
- *Saudi Arabia*: A 2013 survey of students in 30 secondary schools indicated that 97% were receiving private tutoring.

Fewer statistics are available from Palestine, Syria and Yemen, but informal evidence also shows high enrolment rates in those countries. In all countries, subjects in strong demand include mathematics, commonly followed by languages (especially English), and sciences.

Demand and supply

As in other countries around the world, the fundamental driver of demand for private tutoring is social competition. Since performance in schooling is a principal vehicle for such competition, most tutoring is underpinned by a desire to achieve adequate – and preferably high – scores in examinations. Private tutoring helps some students to catch up, and others to get ahead or stay ahead.

Beyond this fundamental driver are specifics related to mainstream schools. Parents and students may identify gaps in the instruction by school teachers and may complain about a lack of individual attention in large classes. Also important are cultural factors, particularly evident among the non-national populations. Thus, families of Egyptian, Indian and Pakistani nationalities, for example, are more likely to receive private tutoring than families of North American, Australasian or European nationalities.

Cultural factors may also shape the supply of tutoring. In Egypt, India and Pakistan, it is common for regular teachers to supplement their salaries through private tutoring, and teachers working in the Middle East who are nationals of those countries bring their cultures with them. A major problem arises when teachers (non-national or national) neglect their regular lessons, or even deliberately cut content in order to promote demand for their supplementary services. Other tutoring is provided by commercial operators, some of whom may provide good quality but others provide questionable quality in unregulated marketplaces.

The impact of shadow education

Academic achievement

An obvious question for both participants and detached analysts is whether shadow education 'works' in raising the achievement scores of its recipients. This simple question does not have a simple answer: much depends on the quality and motivations of the students, and on the quality and pedagogical frameworks of the tutors. Nevertheless, most students and families receiving private tutoring do feel that it assists academic achievement. This perspective is to be expected since families would likely not invest in tutoring if they did not anticipate a benefit. Yet, many students and families feel pressurised to invest in shadow education because everyone else seems to be doing so.

Moreover, a perspective that links private tutoring to schooling shows that such tutoring can subtract as well as supplement. Students may respect their tutors, over whom they have a choice and to whom they are paying money, more than their teachers; and regular teachers may devote less effort when they know that large proportions of their students have separate tutoring as a safety net. In addition, the burden of schooling plus tutoring contributes to tiredness and potential inefficiency for the students.

Social inequalities

It is obvious that rich families can invest in more and better tutoring than can middle-income families, who, in turn, can invest in more and better tutoring than poor families. Private tutoring is thus a major instrument for maintaining and exacerbating social inequalities.

Other forms of inequality are geographic, because tutorial centres are more likely to be available in urban than rural areas. Technology can reduce this geographic imbalance, yet still high-income families are likely to have better access to broadband and updated computer equipment.

Ethics and social values

In some settings, private tutoring has a corrupting element. This is particularly evident when teachers neglect their regular duties in order to devote their energies to private tutoring. Especially problematic are situations in which teachers pressurise their existing students to take supplementary lessons.

More broadly, private tutoring is a part of marketisation of education. It shows that many aspects can be purchased and that government promises of free education cannot always be trusted.

Implications for policy makers

Regulations

Two groups of regulations need particular consideration: (a) for serving teachers who provide private supplementary tutoring and (b) for companies that provide such tutoring.

Among the 12 countries considered, 10 had some sort of regulation concerning provision of private tutoring by serving teachers. The regulations ranged from strict prohibition to approval under certain circumstances. The governments of the remaining two countries were in a laissez-faire category, basically ignoring the phenomenon.

Fewer countries had regulations for commercial tutorial centres other than general regulations applicable to all categories of business. The regulations in Qatar were the most detailed, including focus on premises, tutors' qualifications, prices and class sizes.

For both categories, however, enactment of regulations may be more difficult than preparation of documents. Policy makers need to consider the capacity to implement regulations during the process of designing those regulations.

Making tutoring less necessary

Alongside regulations should be efforts to make private tutoring less necessary. It will never disappear, because families will always be competitive; but policy makers can pay attention to matters of curriculum, including the impact of high-stakes examinations. They can also consider teachers' delivery styles and availability of in-school support for students with diverse needs.

Complementing the aforementioned points about the demand side of tutoring are observations about the supply side. Teachers will feel under less pressure to provide tutoring if they have adequate salaries. Of course, this issue is problematic in the low-income countries, but the matter also deserves attention in the middle- and high-income countries.

Partnerships

The issues of private tutoring cannot be resolved by Ministries of Education by themselves. The study highlights the needs for, and examples of, partnerships with

- other government Ministries,
- subnational levels of government,
- teachers' unions,
- parents,
- schools, and
- the media.

Partnership may even be possible with the tutorial sector itself. In other parts of the world, membership associations have been established for tutoring providers. These associations may dialogue with governments and may set up mechanisms for self-regulation.

Foreword

I write the foreword for this book with great pleasure. It is the first regional study for the Middle East on the very important topic of private supplementary tutoring, widely called shadow education. The RCEP has previously focused on this theme in the UAE (Rocha & Hamed, 2018), and now welcomes this instructive comparative study of the broader region. The authors have liaised closely with RCEP colleagues, and in November 2021, we were proud to host a Policy Forum for representatives from the Ministries of Education in the region together with a wider range of stakeholders, including practitioners, researchers and parents.

The book is an admirable product of partnership in co-authoring. Mark Bray is the leading international figure for comparative research in this field, having written the first global study of the phenomenon for UNESCO's International Institute for Educational Planning (IIEP) in Paris, of which he later became director (Bray, 1999). That initial book has been followed up by regional studies focusing on Africa (Bray, 2021a), Asia (Bray, 2022; Bray & Lykins, 2012), Europe (Bray, 2011, 2021b), the Mediterranean (Bray et al., 2013) and post-Soviet countries (Silova et al., 2006); and alongside these regional works are multiple studies focused on individual countries. For the present book, Mark Bray has co-authored with Anas Hajar, who was able to access the literature in Arabic as well as English. Anas Hajar is at an earlier stage in his career than Mark Bray, yet has already published articles on shadow education in locations as different as England (Hajar, 2018, 2020) and Kazakhstan (Hajar & Abenova, 2021; Hajar et al., 2022). Both authors have also undertaken empirical research on the theme in the UAE, alongside much interaction with stakeholders in other countries of the region through formal and informal channels allied to UNESCO, the League of Arab States and other bodies.

A major theme within the book stresses the importance of context. On the one hand, schools and their shadows have similarities in structures and functions across the globe, that is, not only in the Middle East but also in all other parts of the world. On the other hand are major differences arising from cultural, economic and political forces. Concerning the 12 countries on which the present book focuses, the six members of the GCC form one group in contrast with the other six Arab countries. Yet even within these groups, and within the individual countries, significant contextual diversity contributes to variations in patterns.

At the broadest level, one may ask whether private supplementary tutoring should be viewed positively or negatively. The answer to some extent depends on the role and perspective of the person making the judgement: parents may have different views from school teachers, who in turn may have different views from government personnel. From an economic perspective, private tutoring provides employment for enterprises and for individuals operating informally. Tutoring aims also to contribute to learning, which, in turn, should be a key ingredient for social and economic development. However, private tutoring also maintains and exacerbates social inequalities, and it can have a backwash on the dynamics of mainstream schooling. For these reasons, attention is needed monitoring and perhaps also to active steering of the sector through regulations and other means.

In line with this remark, the authors conclude their book by stressing the overall need to 'take the topic out of the shadows', with public discussion among all stakeholders. Such discussion may be at multiple levels, from school and community at one end to national and supranational at the other end. The UNESCO-RCEP mandate is especially at national and supranational levels of the Middle East region, and we are equally glad to share these analyses with partners across other world regions. This book is a strong demonstration of this approach, and I am confident that it will indeed be welcomed at multiple levels within, across and beyond the 12 countries on which it has specific focus.

Mahra Hilal Almutaiwei
Director, UNESCO Regional Center for Educational Planning (RCEP)
Sharjah, United Arab Emirates

References

Bray, Mark (1999): *The Shadow Education System: Private Tutoring and Its Implications for Planners*. Paris: UNESCO International Institute for Educational Planning (IIEP). https://unesdoc.unesco.org/ark:/48223/pf0000180205/PDF/180205eng.pdf.multi

Bray, Mark (2011): *The Challenge of Shadow Education: Private Tutoring and Its Implications for Policy Makers in the European Union*. Brussels: European Commission. www.nesse.fr/nesse/activities/reports/activities/reports/the-challenge-of-shadow-education-1

Bray, Mark (2021a): *Shadow Education in Africa: Private Supplementary Tutoring and Its Policy Implications*. Hong Kong: Comparative Education Research Centre, The University of Hong Kong. https://cerc.edu.hku.hk/books/shadow-education-in-africa-private-supplementary-tutoring-and-its-policy-implications/

Bray, Mark (2021b): 'Shadow Education in Europe: Growing Prevalence, Underlying Forces, and Policy Implications'. *ECNU Review of Education* [East China Normal University], Vol.4, No.3, pp. 442–475. https://journals.sagepub.com/doi/full/10.1177/2096531119890142

Bray, Mark (2022): 'Shadow Education in Asia and the Pacific: Features and Implications of Private Supplementary Tutoring'. in Lee, Wing On; Brown, Phillip; Goodwin, A. Lin & Green, Andy (eds.), *International Handbook on Education in Asia-Pacific*. Singapore: Springer.

Bray, Mark & Lykins, Chad (2012): *Shadow Education: Private Supplementary Tutoring and Its Implications for Policy Makers in Asia*. Mandaluyong City: Asian Development Bank and Hong Kong: Comparative Education Research Centre, The University of Hong Kong.

Bray, Mark; Mazawi, André E. & Sultana, Ronald G. (eds.) (2013): *Private Tutoring Across the Mediterranean: Power Dynamics, and Implications for Learning and Equity*. Rotterdam: Sense.

Hajar, Anas (2018): 'Exploring Year 6 Pupils' Perceptions of Private Tutoring: Evidence From Three Mainstream Schools in England'. *Oxford Review of Education*, Vol.44, No.4, pp. 514–531.

Hajar, Anas (2020): 'The Association Between Private Tutoring and Access to Grammar Schools: Voices of Year 6 Pupils and Teachers in South-east England'. *British Educational Research Journal*, Vol.46, No.3, pp. 459–479.

Hajar, Anas & Abenova, Saule (2021): 'The Role of Private Tutoring in Admission to Higher Education: Evidence From a Highly Selective University in Kazakhstan'. *Hungarian Educational Research Journal*, Vol.11, No.2, pp. 124–142.

Hajar, Anas; Sagintayeva, Aida & Izekenova, Zhanna (2022): 'Child Participatory Research Methods: Exploring Grade 6 Pupils' Experiences of Private Tutoring in Kazakhstan'. *Cambridge Journal of Education*, DOI: 10.1080/0305764X.2021.2004088.

Rocha, Valeria & Hamed, Sheren (2018): *Parents' Perspectives on Paid Private Tutoring in the United Arab Emirates*. Sharjah: UNESCO Regional Center for Educational Planning.

Silova, Iveta; Būdienė, Virginija & Bray, Mark (eds.) (2006): *Education in a Hidden Marketplace: Monitoring of Private Tutoring*. New York: Open Society Institute. www.opensocietyfoundations.org/uploads/394bb3b8-ef04-4f5f-8521-5e0b4dff389c/hidden_20070216.pdf

1 Introduction

Private supplementary tutoring has become increasingly visible across the globe. The Middle East is no exception, though in the international literature patterns in the region have been less documented than elsewhere. This study maps the phenomenon in the Middle East, highlighting its scale, nature and policy implications. Many of the relevant policy makers are in national Ministries of Education, but the book also has pertinence for policy makers at sub-national and school levels.

In this mapping approach, the work resembles and complements other regional studies focusing, for example, on Africa (Bray, 2021a), East Asia (Zhang & Yamato, 2018), South Asia (Joshi, 2021), Europe (Bray, 2021b), the Mediterranean (Bray et al., 2013) and post-Soviet states (Silova, 2009; Silova et al., 2006). These regional studies drew on multiple national studies, and sat alongside a few global studies (e.g. Entrich, 2021; Park et al., 2016; Zhang & Bray, 2020). The present study shows both commonalities and differences with other regions, adding an important component to deepening understanding of the global picture. Particular emphasis is placed on sociopolitical interpretations of the nature and roles of private tutoring, which add to conceptual insights not only for the Middle East but also more broadly.

An initial challenge has been to define the Middle East, recognising the existence of multiple approaches (see, e.g. Hinnebusch, 2003; Lewis, 1998). The book has been prepared in collaboration with UNESCO's RCEP in Sharjah, UAE. RCEP was established in 2003 primarily to serve the six member-states of the GCC plus Yemen, and also provides much leadership across the Arabic-speaking countries of the Middle East and North Africa (MENA). Since private tutoring in North Africa is addressed in the 2021 study that also focuses on Sub-Saharan Africa (Bray, 2021a), the present work focuses on the 12 countries of the Middle East that employ Arabic as the (or an) official language.[1] These countries are Bahrain, Iraq, Jordan, Kuwait, Lebanon, Oman, Palestine, Qatar, Saudi Arabia, Syria, the UAE and Yemen.

DOI: 10.4324/9781003317593-1

2 *Introduction*

The study is primarily based on published literature, supplemented by information obtained through RCEP,[2] and by formal and informal interviews of various kinds. The literature on which the study draws is in English and Arabic, accessed through library searches, Google, follow-up of references and interchanges with professional colleagues. The authors particularly sought scholarly works and official documents but also drew on media commentaries of various kinds. The study also draws on documentation and associated discussion during a regional seminar on private tutoring in Arabic-speaking countries attended by researchers and government personnel.[3] Further, the authors' empirical research in the UAE (as well as in many other countries outside the region) has been supplemented by many professional discussions in neighbouring countries.[4]

To set the framework, the study commences with global literature on private tutoring and the sociopolitical forces that shape and are shaped by it. It then turns to contexts in the countries under review, and to data on the scale and features of private tutoring. Much of the picture from the available data is patchy, and among major needs identified by this study is improved and more extensive data collection by governments, academics and others. Nevertheless, even patchy data permit identification of the contours in educational and social impact of private tutoring, particularly when the Middle East data are considered in conjunction with pictures from other world regions; and, in turn, it is possible to identify many implications for policies. These implications are examined in the penultimate chapter, and the final chapter concludes with remarks about what the study adds to broader literatures and to conceptual understanding.

Notes

1 In Iraq, Kurdish is an official language alongside Arabic.
2 This included distribution of a questionnaire to Ministries of Education and the hosting of a November 2021 Policy Forum. Particularly useful were the questionnaire responses from Oman, Jordan, Kuwait and Yemen, and then inputs during the Policy Forum from Ministry personnel from Bahrain, Iraq, Jordan, Kuwait, Syria and the UAE.
3 This event was hosted in Cairo by the General Secretariat of the League of Arab States, 12–13 November 2012, with a lead role played by Mark Bray. In addition to analysing new data from around the region, the event launched the Arabic translation of Bray's book *Confronting the Shadow Education System: What Government Policies for What Private Tutoring?*, of which the English version had been published in 2009 by IIEP.
4 In-country discussions have been held by one or both authors in Bahrain, Kuwait, Qatar, Syria and the UAE, and have been supplemented by counterpart discussions at various regional and global meetings.

References

Bray, Mark (2021a): *Shadow Education in Africa: Private Supplementary Tutoring and Its Policy Implications*. Hong Kong: Comparative Education Research Centre, The University of Hong Kong. https://cerc.edu.hku.hk/books/shadow-education-in-africa-private-supplementary-tutoring-and-its-policy-implications/

Bray, Mark (2021b): 'Shadow Education in Europe: Growing Prevalence, Underlying Forces, and Policy Implications'. *ECNU Review of Education* [East China Normal University], Vol.4, No.3, pp. 442–475. https://journals.sagepub.com/doi/full/10.1177/2096531119890142

Bray, Mark; Mazawi, André E. & Sultana, Ronald G. (eds.) (2013): *Private Tutoring Across the Mediterranean: Power Dynamics, and Implications for Learning and Equity*. Rotterdam: Sense.

Entrich, Steve (2021): 'Worldwide Shadow Education and Social Inequality: Explaining the Differences in the Socioeconomic Gap in Access to Shadow Education Across 63 Societies'. *International Journal of Comparative Sociology*, Vol.61, No.6, pp. 441–475.

Hinnebusch, Raymond (2003): *The International Politics of the Middle East*. Manchester: Manchester University Press.

Joshi, Priyadarshani (2021): 'Private Schooling and Tutoring at Scale in South Asia'. in Sarangapani, Padma M. & Pappu, Rekha (eds.), *Handbook of Education Systems in South Asia*. Singapore: Springer, pp. 1127–1146.

Lewis, Bernard (1998): *The Multiple Identities of the Middle East*. New York: Schocken.

Park, Hyunjoon; Buchmann, Claudia; Choi, Jaesung & Merry, Joseph J. (2016): 'Learning Beyond the School Walls: Trends and Implications'. *Annual Review of Sociology*, Vol.42, pp. 231–252.

Silova, Iveta (ed.) (2009): *Private Supplementary Tutoring in Central Asia: New Opportunities and Burdens*. Paris: UNESCO International Institute for Educational Planning (IIEP). www.iiep.unesco.org/en/publication/private-supplementary-tutoring-central-asia-new-opportunities-and-burdens

Silova, Iveta; Būdienė, Virginija & Bray, Mark (eds.) (2006): *Education in a Hidden Marketplace: Monitoring of Private Tutoring*. New York: Open Society Institute. www.opensocietyfoundations.org/uploads/394bb3b8-ef04-4f5f-8521-5e0b4dff389c/hidden_20070216.pdf

Zhang, Wei & Bray, Mark (2020): 'Comparative Research on Shadow Education: Achievements, Challenges, and the Agenda Ahead'. *European Journal of Education*, Vol.55, No.3, pp. 322–341.

Zhang, Wei & Yamato, Yoko (2018): 'Shadow Education in East Asia: Entrenched but Evolving Private Supplementary Tutoring'. in Kennedy, Kerry & Lee, John C.K. (eds.), *Routledge International Handbook on Schools and Schooling in Asia*. London: Routledge, pp. 323–332.

2 Global perspectives on shadow education

Definitions and scope

Several definitional points are needed to set the ground for the present study. First, some people interpret the word 'tutoring' to imply one-to-one or possibly small-group instruction. This is included in the concept for the present study, but tutoring is also taken to include full classes, sometimes even in lecture-theatres serving hundreds of students, and various forms of online instruction.

Second, the study is concerned with tutoring provided as a supplement rather than an alternative to schooling. Thus, it focuses on extra instruction received by pupils who are already registered in schools. The study is principally concerned with academic subjects such as languages, mathematics, sciences and other examinable domains. Some authors (e.g. Buchmann et al., 2010; Malik, 2017) have employed broader foci to include musical, artistic, or sporting skills which are learned primarily for pleasure or for more rounded personal development, but they are beyond the focus of the present work.

Third, this study is concerned with private provision, meaning instruction in exchange for a fee. Usually, this means a cash payment, though sometimes remuneration may be in goods or services.

In the literature, private supplementary tutoring is commonly called shadow education on the grounds that it mimics schooling (see, e.g. Aurini et al., 2013; Bray, 1999, 2009; Kim & Jung, 2021). Thus, as the curriculum changes in the schools, so it changes in the shadow; and as school systems expand, so do shadow systems. The metaphor is also used in the title of this book, but the authors recognise that it cannot always be applied tightly. Thus, while some forms of private tutoring use the same textbooks as the schools, others go beyond these textbooks with expanded visions. Likewise, the metaphor implies that students first learn material in their schools and then reinforce or expand their learning through tutoring. However, in some

DOI: 10.4324/9781003317593-2

settings, the tutoring comes first, with students securing a 'head start' and then repeating material during their school lessons.

Within school systems, the focus is on primary and secondary education. Private tutoring may also be supplied in pre-primary and post-secondary education, but these levels raise different issues and are beyond the scope of this study.

Providers and modes

Three main categories of private-tutoring providers may be discerned around the world. First are full-time teachers in both public and private schools who offer tutoring on a part-time basis to earn extra incomes. Second are enterprises established for the purpose, in some cases relatively informal and perhaps not paying taxes but in other cases officially registered with the authorities. Most enterprises are small, but some operate nationally and even internationally through branches, franchises or cyberspace. The third category embraces self-employed providers operating on an informal basis. Around the world, many university students and even some secondary students earn extra pocket money through private tutoring. Other self-employed providers include individuals who have identified market niches to offer their services on either full-time or part-time bases. They may be in all age groups, ranging from recent school/university leavers to retirees.

The modes of tutoring provision may be very varied (Figure 2.1). Most obvious is face-to-face provision in the homes of the tutors or the students, in public locations such as libraries and cafés, and in purpose-built premises such as tutorial centres. Alongside these long-standing modes are new ones permitted by technological developments and in many countries accelerated by the needs for social distancing imposed by the Covid-19 pandemic that hit the world in 2020. Thus, tutoring may be delivered online in live, mixed or recorded modes, again serving students on a one-to-one, small-group or large-class basis, and perhaps even serving thousands at a single time.

Related to these modes is the timing of provision. In most settings, tutoring takes place before or after school hours, at weekends, and during vacations. Sometimes, however, tutoring is provided during school hours either with school approval or, more commonly, without it. In the latter case, students may skip schooling in order to attend tutoring (see, e.g. Altinyelken, 2013, p. 199; Bhorkar & Bray, 2018, p. 149; Silova & Kazimzade, 2006, p. 128).

Seasonal variations may also be evident. Demand for tutoring often intensifies as students approach important examinations and then abruptly subsides for some time (see, e.g. Bray, 2013a). Alternatively, tutors may

6 *Global perspectives on shadow education*

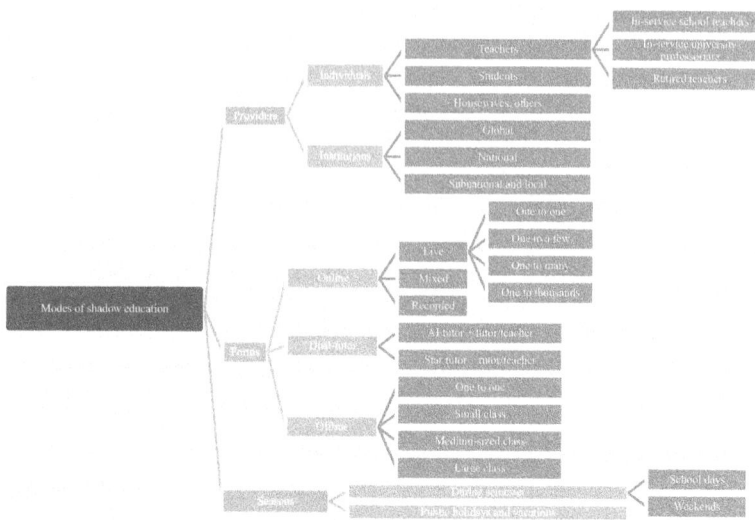

Figure 2.1 Diversity of Modes of Shadow Education Delivery.
Source: Zhang & Bray (2020), p.328.

be active during the long vacations before commencement of the academic year, in order to keep students productively occupied with academic focus and to prepare them for the school lessons ahead (see, e.g. Andrew et al., 2016; Jinga & Ganga, 2012).

Geographic and cultural variations

Private supplementary tutoring is not a new phenomenon. It has likely been received in some social classes since the advent of formal schooling, and has been documented in various countries at least since the 19th century. In Russia, for example, Mikhaylova (2019) has identified newspaper advertisements by private supplementary tutors in the mid-19th century; and in India counterpart advertisements during the 1890s for home tutors to serve upper-class households have been identified by Majumdar (2018). Likewise in Greece, Tsiloglu (2005) documented the emergence of tutorial institutions called *frontistiria* towards the end of the 19th century; and in Japan, Sato (2012) has recorded the parallel development of *jukus* since the early 20th century. In the very different context of Mauritius, Foondun (2002, p. 488) quoted a 1901 comment about private supplementary tutoring received by students in what was then the only state secondary school for boys.

However, only in the second half of the 20th century did the phenomenon emerge in a major way, most obviously in East Asia and particularly in Japan and the Republic of Korea (Harnisch, 1994; Kim, 2016; Rohlen, 1980; Seth, 2002). Enrolment rates have remained high in both countries. Kimura (2018) reported *juku* enrolment rates in Tokyo of 33.7% in elementary, 51.9% in lower secondary, and 29.3% in upper secondary schooling; and Korean statistics indicated 2019 national enrolment rates in private tutoring of 83.5% in elementary, 71.4% in middle, and 67.9% in general high schooling (KOSIS, 2020). Enrolment rates have also long been striking in Hong Kong and Taiwan (Yung & Bray, 2017; Zhan, 2014), and during the 2000s and 2010s, much expanded in Mainland China (Zhang & Bray, 2021). A 2017 household survey by the China Institute for Educational Finance Research (CIEFR) reported regional private tutoring enrolment rates of 60.8% in north-eastern Mainland China, 38.1% in the east, 38.0% in the centre, and 30.5% in the west (Wei, 2018).[1]

Many researchers (e.g. Feng, 2021; Ho, 2010) have attributed high enrolment rates in East Asia to Confucian values of diligence and respect for education. These perspectives have some validity, but the fact that private tutoring is also vigorous in other cultures shows that other factors are pertinent. Thus, for example:

- In *England and Wales*, the Sutton Trust's (2019) national survey found that private tutoring had been received at some time by 27% of sampled students aged 11–16, with the figure reaching 41% in London.
- In *India*, a 2017/18 national survey found that 20% of students across all grades were receiving private tutoring, with the proportion in West Bengal state reaching 75% (India, 2020, p. 113).
- In *Mauritius*, 81% of nationally sampled Grade 6 students were receiving private tutoring in 2013 (Dwarkan, 2017, p. 37).
- In *Greece*, a 2017/18 national sample of final-year students in academic secondary schools found that 85% were receiving private tutoring (Katsillis, 2021, p. 115).

At the same time, the world displays low as well as high spots. The Nordic region has long been a low spot, reflecting its strong social welfare systems and trust in public schooling. Yet recent times have brought significant expansion of private tutoring in the Nordic countries (Christensen & Zhang, 2021) even if enrolment rates remain below 10%. Southern Africa appeared to have low rates of tutoring as measured by the 2007 survey of the Southern and Eastern Africa Consortium for Monitoring Educational Quality (SACMEQ); but in Eswatini, for example, reported enrolment rates for Grade 6 students increased from 1% in 2007 to 11% in 2013 (Bray, 2021a, p. 17).

Over the same time period, reported rates in Namibia expanded from 3% to 6%, and in South Africa they expanded from 4% to 29%. Driving forces for the growth included entrepreneurs identifying market opportunities, and thus expanded supply as well as expanded demand.

Patterns of Egypt have particular pertinence because they have much influence in the 12 Middle East countries on which the study mainly focuses. Shadow education, particularly that delivered by teachers as a supplementary occupation, has been a significant phenomenon in Egypt since the mid-20th century. As long ago as 1947, the government felt it necessary to pass regulations that prohibited teachers – somewhat ineffectively, as it turned out – from providing private lessons without permission from their schools and the Ministry of Education (Egypt, 1947). Yet low salaries pushed teachers to find mechanisms to supplement their incomes, and private tutoring became a norm. As noted by Cook and El-Refaee (2016), by the mid-1990s private tutoring had become an industry with revenue estimated equivalent to US$2 billion. Teachers, they added (p. 297), 'were paid so poorly (on average less than $100 per month) that they simply had to supplement their income with tutoring in order to make ends meet'. Despite policy initiatives to address the situation (see, e.g. Bahaa el Din, 1997, p. 99), the practice in Egypt continued unabated. A 2012 national survey reported that 33%

Box 2.1   Perceptions of Incidence – the Arab Region and Beyond

In 1995, Qatar's Minister of Education and Culture, Mohammad Abdel Rahim Kafoud (quoted by Hasan, 1996, p. 45), stated that private tutoring 'only exists in certain Arab countries'. Presumably he included Qatar on this list, and probably also Egypt, Kuwait and Saudi Arabia. But he was mistaken in his impression that private tutoring did not exist elsewhere. It was firmly grounded in parts of East Asia and also in countries as diverse as Greece, India and Mauritius.

Yet despite these historical patterns and subsequent expansion, general awareness and accompanying discussion about private tutoring are limited both in the Arab countries and more widely. This observation underlines the need both to undertake and to disseminate more research. Data cited in the present study (and elsewhere) about private tutoring in other world regions can help expand awareness in the Arab countries; and by corollary, discussions in the present study can help readers elsewhere to know more about the Arab region.

of students even in Grade 1 were receiving private (one-to-one) lessons, and that a further 9% were in fee-paying help groups; in Grade these numbers were 6, 61% and 12%; in Grade they were 9, 64% and 10%; and in Grade they were 12, 56% and 2% (Assaad & Krafft, 2015, p. 24).

Positives and negatives

On the positive side, private tutoring can help slow learners to keep up with peers. In Rwanda, Nayebare (2013) highlighted the value of a 'hustle free studying environment' in one-to-one tutoring that can especially support introverted students. Some types of group tutoring can also help slow learners; and the benefits extend beyond the learners themselves to their families, schools and the wider society. Teachers in the classroom setting benefit when slow learners keep up with their peers, not only because other people (i.e. the tutors) are providing support but also because that support reduces disparities in the regular classrooms.

At the other end of the scale, private tutoring also serves high achievers. In this case, the tutoring is more likely to exacerbate disparities in classrooms, but it commonly stretches the high achievers in productive ways. Again in the Rwandan context, Nayebare quoted a student receiving tutoring who wanted not just to be good but able when the national examinations came to be 'perfect in each and every area of the subjects we are doing'. Beyond the narrow focus of examinations, such stretching can contribute to motivation and to both personal and social development.

Private tutoring also provides employment and incomes. Employees may be full-time or part-time in tutorial centres and in supporting occupations such as advertising and book production. The Republic of Korea experienced noteworthy expansion following the turn of the century. The annual increase in the number of private tutors between 2001 and 2006 was approximately 7.1%, and by 2009, the sector was reported to be the largest employer of graduates from the humanities and social sciences (Kim & Park, 2013, p. 273).

Further, the extra incomes may be substantial for teachers undertaking tutoring alongside their main duties. In Cambodia, a 2013/14 sample of secondary teachers reported monthly incomes from tutoring averaging 596,000 riels (US$166), which meant that these teachers were in effect earning almost as much from tutoring as from their official salaries averaging 633,000 riels (Bray et al., 2016, p. 294). Patterns were even more striking in Sri Lanka, where graduate government teachers in 2007 received monthly salaries of 12,000 to 15,000 rupees (US$108–135) but could earn 1,100 rupees per hour from tutoring. One teacher quoted by Samath (2007) observed: 'What I get a month from my government job can be earned in 3 or 4 days [of tutoring]'. Such patterns even had an indirect benefit for the authorities managing the education system. The arrangement helped to keep teachers in the profession despite low official salaries.

However, private tutoring by default maintains and exacerbates social inequalities because prosperous families can secure more and better-quality tutoring than families with lower incomes. In England and Wales, for example, Holloway and Kirby (2020, p. 173) noted survey statistics showing that 31.2% of children from highly affluent backgrounds had received private tutoring compared with 20.6% from medium-affluence households and 15.5% from low-affluence households; and compounding these quantitative disparities presumably were qualitative ones. Similar patterns have been identified in societies as different as Japan and Egypt (Entrich, 2018; Sieverding et al., 2019), and may be taken as a universal phenomenon. Yet issues still arise when tutoring enrolment rates are substantial among low-income households. The financial burden is likely to be heavy; and when private tutoring becomes the norm, families either have to find ways to invest in it alongside others or face the prospect of being left out of the race altogether.

Further issues arise when serving teachers provide supplementary tutoring. In particular, they may be tempted to neglect their regular classes, for which they have standardised payment regardless of quality, in order to devote effort to their private tutoring. Even more problematic, teachers who tutor their existing students may deliberately cut content from their regular classes in order to promote demand for private tutoring (Bray, 2013b; 2021b). This is what Jayachandran (2014) has called 'incentives to perform badly'.

Supply and demand are obviously linked to each other in tutoring as much as in other domains. In many settings, supply creates demand – because families invest in tutoring when it is available, perhaps further motivated by the perception that most peers are investing in it and by fear of being left behind. Writing about Japan, Dierkes (2013) has highlighted ways that companies market their services by stoking anxieties in what he calls an 'insecurity industry'. Ball and Youdell (2008, p. 98) have similarly noted that specialist childhood and parenting magazines 'thrive on both the commercial exploitation of anxiety and childhood generally as a new market opportunity'. This is related to hidden social dynamics that shift the burdens of responsibility, security and risk management from the state to the parents (Doherty & Dooley, 2018).

Elaborating, social competition is a key driver of demand for tutoring in societies of all kinds – both prosperous and impoverished. Intensified by the forces of globalisation, families increasingly feel that schooling is not by itself sufficient in the efforts to achieve social mobility or to retain existing social status in the middle and upper classes. Some families invest in shadow education to compensate for perceived inadequacies of schooling, while others recognise that the schooling is good but still want more. This factor helps to explain why private tutoring is prevalent not only in poorly resourced education systems, such as those of Bangladesh and Zimbabwe (Mahmud, 2021; Bukaliya, 2019), but also in well-resourced societies such as Germany and Singapore (Guill et al., 2020; Teo & Koh, 2020). Some families also seek private tutoring to keep their children gainfully occupied outside schooling hours, and to 'outsource' the stresses of supervising homework. Again such factors are evident in societies as diverse as France (Oller & Glasman, 2013) and Togo (Amouzou-Glikpa, 2018).

Note

1   However, fierce regulations issued by China's central government in 2021 (China, 2021) greatly reduced supply of private tutoring, at least in the short run.

References

Altinyelken, Hülya Koşar (2013): 'The Demand for Private Tutoring in Turkey: Unintended Consequences of Curriculum Reform'. in Bray, Mark; Mazawi, André E. & Sultana, Ronald G. (eds.), *Private Tutoring across the Mediterranean: Power Dynamics and Implications for Learning and Equity*. Rotterdam: Sense, pp. 187–204.

Amouzou-Glikpa, Amévor (2018): 'Le phénomène des cours de répétition: Quelle lecture des dynamiques sociales dans le secteur de l'éducation au Togo?'. *EDUCOM: Revue du Centre d'Études et de Recherches sur les Organisations, la Communication et l'Éducation (CEROCE) de l'Université de Lomé*, No. 8, pp. 110–135.

Andrew, Kipsang; Saina, Christopher; Kimurgor, Boit J. & Taalam, Barnabas (2016): 'Teachers' Justifications for the Need for Holiday Coaching in Kenya: Syllabus Coverage and Other Factors'. *International Journal of Academic Research and Development*, Vol.1, No.9, pp. 61–68.

Assaad, Ragui & Krafft, Caroline (2015): 'Is Free Basic Education in Egypt a Reality or a Myth?'. *International Journal of Educational Development*, Vol.45, No.1, pp. 16–30.

Aurini, Janice; Davies, Scott & Dierkes, Julian (eds.) (2013): *Out of the Shadows: The Global Intensification of Supplementary Education*. Bingley: Emerald.

Bahaa el Din, Hussein Kamal (1997): *Education and the Future*. Kalyoub: Al-Ahram Commercial Presses.

Ball, Stephen J. & Youdell, Deborah (2008): *Hidden Privatisation in Public Education*. Brussels: Education International. https://issuu.com/educationinternational/docs/hidden-privatisation

Bhorkar, Shalini & Bray, Mark (2018): 'The Expansion and Roles of Private Tutoring in India: From Supplementation to Supplantation'. *International Journal of Educational Development*, Vol.62, pp. 148–156.

Bray, Mark (1999): *The Shadow Education System: Private Tutoring and Its Implications for Planners*. Paris: UNESCO International Institute for Educational Planning (IIEP). https://unesdoc.unesco.org/ark:/48223/pf0000180205/PDF/180205eng.pdf.multi

Bray, Mark (2009): *Confronting the Shadow Education System: What Government Policies for What Private Tutoring?*. Paris: UNESCO International Institute for Educational Planning (IIEP). www.iiep.unesco.org/en/confronting-shadow-education-system-what-government-policies-what-private-tutoring-12159 [Arabic version: https://unesdoc.unesco.org/ark:/48223/pf0000185106_ara/PDF/185106ara.pdf.multi]

Bray, Mark (2013a): 'Benefits and Tensions of Shadow Education: Comparative Perspectives on the Roles and Impact of Private Supplementary Tutoring in the Lives of Hong Kong Students'. *Journal of International and Comparative Education*, Vol.2, No.1, pp. 18–30.

Bray, Mark (2013b): 'Shadow Education: The Rise of Private Tutoring and Associated Corruption Risks'. in Transparency International (ed.), *Global Corruption Report: Education*. London: Routledge, pp. 83–87. www.transparency.org/en/publications/global-corruption-report-education [Arabic version: www.transparency.org/ar/publications/global-corruption-report-education]

Bray, Mark (2021a): *Shadow Education in Africa: Private Supplementary Tutoring and Its Policy Implications*. Hong Kong: Comparative Education Research Centre, The University of Hong Kong. https://cerc.edu.hku.hk/books/shadow-education-in-africa-private-supplementary-tutoring-and-its-policy-implications/

Bray, Mark (2021b): 'Swimming Against the Tide: Comparative Lessons from Government Efforts to Prohibit Private Supplementary Tutoring Delivered by Regular Teachers'. *Hungarian Educational Research Journal*, Vol.11, No.2, pp. 168–188.

Bray, Mark; Kobakhidze, Nutsa; Liu Junyan & Zhang Wei (2016): 'The Internal Dynamics of Privatised Public Education: Fee-charging Supplementary Tutoring Provided by Teachers in Cambodia'. *International Journal of Educational Development*, Vol.49, pp. 291–299.

Buchmann, Claudia; Condron, Dennis J. & Roscigno, Vincent J. (2010): 'Shadow Education, American Style: Test Preparation, the SAT and College Enrollment'. *Social Forces*, Vol.89, No.2, pp. 435–462.

Bukaliya, Richard (2019): 'The Social Role of Extra Lessons in Zimbabwean High Density Secondary Schools'. *Sumerianz Journal of Education, Linguistics and Literature*, Vol.2, No.12, pp. 162–174.

Christensen, Søren & Zhang, Wei (eds.) (2021): *Shadow Education in the Nordic Countries*. Special issue of *ECNU Review of Education* [East China Normal University], Vol.4, No.3. www.roe.ecnu.edu.cn/f9/1d/c12911a391453/page.htm

Cook, Bradley J. & El-Refaee, Engy (2016): 'Egypt: A Perpetual Reform Agenda', in Kirdar, Serra (ed.), *Education in the Arab World*. London: Bloomsbury, pp. 285–305.

Egypt, Ministry of Education (1947): *'The Organisation of Private [Supplementary] Lessons for Students'. Ministerial Circular No.7530*. Cairo: Ministry of Education. [in Arabic]

Dierkes, Julian (2013): 'The Insecurity Industry: Supplementary Education in Japan', in Aurini, Janice; Davies, Scott & Dierkes, Julian (eds.), *Out of the Shadows: The Global Intensification of Supplementary Education*. Bingley: Emerald, pp. 3–21.

Doherty, Catherine & Dooley, Karen (2018): 'Responsibilising Parents: The Nudge towards Shadow Tutoring'. *British Journal of Sociology of Education*, Vol.39, No.4, pp. 551–566.

Dwarkan, L. (2017): *SACMEQ IV Study Mauritius: A Study of the Conditions of Schooling and the Quality of Education*. Port Louis: Southern and Eastern Africa Consortium for Monitoring Educational Quality (SACMEQ).

Entrich, Steve R. (2018): *Shadow Education and Social Inequalities in Japan: Evolving Patterns and Conceptual Implications*. Cham: Springer.

Foondun, A. Raffick (2002): The Issue of Private Tuition: An Analysis of the Practice in Mauritius and Selected South-East Asian Countries. *International Review of Education*, Vol.48, No.6, pp. 485–515.

Harnisch, Delwyn L. (1994): 'Supplemental Education in Japan: *Juku* Schooling and its Implication'. *Journal of Curriculum Studies*, Vol. 26, No.3, pp. 323–334.

Hasan, Muhammad Siddiq Muhammad (1996, reprinted 2019): 'The Phenomenon of Private Tutoring: Diagnosis and Treatment'. *Al-Tarbiya Magazine*, Vol.48, Issue 196, pp. 44–58. [in Arabic]

Ho, Nga Hon (2010): 'Hong Kong's Shadow Education: Private Tutoring in Hong Kong'. *The Hong Kong Anthropologist*, Vol.4, pp. 62–85.

Holloway, Sarah L. & Kirby, Philip (2020): 'Neoliberalising Education: New Geographies of Private Tuition, Class Privilege, and Minority Ethnic Advancement'. *Antipode: A Radical Journal of Geography*, Vol.52, No.1, pp. 164–184.

Feng, Siyuan (2021): 'The Evolution of Shadow Education in China: From Emergence to Capitalisation'. *Hungarian Educational Research Journal*, Vol.11, No.2, pp. 89–100.

Guill, Karin; Lüdtke, Oliver & Köller, Olaf (2020): 'Assessing the Instructional Quality of Private Tutoring and Its Effects on Student Outcomes: Analyses From the German National Educational Panel Study'. *British Journal of Educational Psychology*, Vol.90, pp. 282–300.

India, National Statistical Office (2020): *Household Social Consumption on Education in India: NSS 75th Round, July 2017-June 2018*. New Delhi: National Statistical Office. www.mospi.gov.in/sites/default/files/NSS75252E/KI_Education_75th_Final.pdf

Jayachandran, Seema (2014): 'Incentives to Teach Badly: After-School Tutoring in Developing Countries'. *Journal of Development Economics*, Vol.108, pp. 190–205.

Jinga, Nyaradzo & Ganga, Emily (2012): 'Effects of Holiday Lessons and Financial Pressures on Low-Income Families and Households in Masvingo, Zimbabwe'. *Journal of Emerging Trends in Educational Research and Policy Studies*, Vol.2, No.6, pp. 465–470.

Katsillis, Michail (2021): *Factors and Processes of Educational and Social Stratification in Greece: The Role of Shadow Education*. DPhil thesis, University of Oxford.

Kim, Kyung-Min & Park, Daekwon (2013): 'Impacts of Urban Economic Factors on Private Tutoring Industry'. *Asia Pacific Education Review*, Vol.13, No.2, pp. 273–280.

Kim, Young-Chun (2016): *Shadow Education and the Curriculum and Culture of Schooling in South Korea*. New York: Palgrave Macmillan.

Kim, Young-Chun & Jung, Jung-Hoon (eds.) (2021): *Theorizing Shadow Education and Academic Success in East Asia: Understanding the Meaning, Value, and Use of Shadow Education by East Asian Students*. New York: Routledge.

Kimura, Haruo (2018): *Data-based Discussion on Education and Children in Japan 2: Analyzing Juku -Another School after School*. Tokyo: Child Research Net. www.childresearch.net/projects/data_Japan/2018_02.html#:~:text=The%20 juku%20enrollment%20rate%20falls,during%202nd%20and%203rd%20grade, accessed 19 February 2021.

KOSIS [Korean Statistical Information Service] (2020): 'Participation Rate on Private Education by School Level and Characteristics'. http://kosis.kr/eng/statisticsList/statisticsListIndex.do?menuId=M_01_01&vwcd=MT_ETITLE&parm TabId=M_01_01&statId=1963003&themaId=#SelectStatsBoxDiv, accessed 19 February 2021.

Malik, Muhammad Abid (2017): 'Shadow Education: Evolution, Flaws and Further Development of the Term'. *Social Sciences and Education Research Review*, Vol.4, No.1, pp. 6–29.

Mahmud, Rafsan (2021): 'Family Socioeconomic Determinants and Students' Demand for Private Supplementary Tutoring in English in Urban and Rural Bangladesh'. *Education and Urban Society*, Vol.57, No.7, pp. 831–851.

Majumdar, Manabi (2018): 'Access, Success, and Excess: Debating Shadow Education in India', in Kumar, Krishna (ed.), *Routledge Handbook of Education in India: Debates, Practices, and Policies*. London: Routledge, pp. 273–284.

Mikhaylova, Tatiana (2019): 'Shadow education – Russian edition'. Presentation to the First Meeting of Asian Scandinavian Network on Shadow Education, Danish School of Education, Aarhus University, Copenhagen.

Nayebare, Irene (2013): 'Private Tutoring is Here to Stay'. *The New Times* [Rwanda], 20 March. www.newtimes.co.rw/section/read/64041, accessed 25 February 2021.

Oller, Claudine & Glasman, Dominique (2013): 'Education as a Market in France: Forms and Stakes of Private Tutoring', in Bray, Mark; Mazawi, André E. & Sultana, Ronald G. (eds.), *Private Tutoring across the Mediterranean: Power Dynamics and Implications for Learning and Equity*. Rotterdam: Sense, pp. 77–91.

Rohlen, Thomas P. (1980): 'The *Juku* Phenomenon: An Exploratory Essay'. *Journal of Japanese Studies*, Vol.6, No.2, pp. 207–242.

Samath, Feizal (2007): 'Sri Lanka: Primary Education in Crisis'. *Inter Press Service News Agency*, 19 June. www.ipsnews.net/2007/06/sri-lanka-primary-education-in-crisis/ accessed 25 February 2021.

Sato, Yuji (ed.) (2012): *One Hundred Years of Juku and Fifty Years of Juku Associations*. Tokyo: Federation of Private Tutoring Associations. [in Japanese]

Seth, Michael J. (2002): *Education Fever: Society, Politics, and the Pursuit of Schooling in South Korea*. Honolulu: University of Hawai'i Press.

Sieverding, Maia; Krafft, Caroline & Elbadawy, Asmaa (2019): 'An Exploration of the Drivers of Private Tutoring in Egypt'. *Comparative Education Review*, Vol.63, No.4, pp. 562–590.

Silova, Iveta & Elmina Kazimzade (2006): 'Azerbaijan', in Silova, Iveta; Būdienė, Virginija & Bray, Mark (eds.), *Education in a Hidden Marketplace: Monitoring of Private Tutoring*. New York: Open Society Institute, pp. 113–141. www.opensocietyfoundations.org/uploads/394bb3b8-ef04-4f5f-8521-5e0b4dff389c/hidden_20070216.pdf

Sutton Trust (2019). Private tuition polling 2019. www.suttontrust.com/wp-content/uploads/2019/12/PrivateTuition2019-PollingTables.pdf and www.suttontrust.com/news-opinion/all-news-opinion/one-in-four-teachers-take-on-private-tuition-outside-of-school.

Teo, Peter & Koh, Dorothy (2020): 'Shadow Education in Singapore: A Deweyan Perspective'. *Educational Philosophy and Theory*, Vol.52, No.8, pp. 869–879.

Tsiloglu, Lefteris (2005): *Frontistiria in Greece: History and People*. Athens: Kedros. [in Greek]

Yung, Kevin Wai-Ho & Bray, Mark (2017): 'Shadow Education: Features, Expansion and Implications', in Tse, Kwan-Choi Thomas & Lee, Michael H. (eds.), *Making Sense of Education in Post-Handover Hong Kong: Achievements and Challenges*. London: Routledge, pp. 95–111.

Wei, Yi (2018): *The 2017 Chinese Family Survey of Educational Expenditure*. Beijing: China Institute of Education Finance Research. [in Chinese] http://ciefr.pku.edu.cn/cbw/kyjb/2018/03/kyjb_5257.shtml

Zhan, Shengli (2014): 'The Private Tutoring Industry in Taiwan: Government Policies and their Implementation'. *Asia Pacific Journal of Education*, Vol.34, No.4, pp. 492–504.

Zhang, Wei & Bray, Mark (2020): 'Comparative Research on Shadow Education: Achievements, Challenges, and the Agenda Ahead'. *European Journal of Education*, Vol.55, No.3, pp. 322–341.

Zhang, Wei & Bray, Mark (2021): 'A Changing Environment of Urban Education: Historical and Spatial Analysis of Private Supplementary Tutoring in China'. *Environment and Urbanization*, Vol. 33, No. 1, pp. 43–62.

3 Middle East contexts

Educational and cultural commonalities

Since this is a study of education, perhaps the greatest significant commonality for present purposes is operation of the globalised model for schooling – albeit with variations – with primary and secondary sections, grades, term-times/vacations, classrooms, trained teachers, and examinations at watershed points. Accompanying this commonality are administrative structures with Ministries of Education at the top, various intermediate bodies depending on the sizes of the countries, and school administrations headed by principals. Such features are so standardised across the globe that they are often taken for granted. Their existence may be illustrated by the fact that Ofori-Attah's (2008) book entitled *Going to School in the Middle East and North Africa* appeared in a series entitled The Global School Room – though even that book seemed to feel that the globalised features did not deserve specific comment. The fact that the countries addressed by the current study all operate standard models for schooling, and do so within labour markets that reward certain types of academic achievement, means that many features of private tutoring in other parts of the world have pertinence to the Middle East, and vice versa.

Beyond this global commonality in the nature of schooling, the 12 countries share cultural features. Among the most significant is the role of Arabic, which shapes peer groups and information flows. Also, in all countries, Islam is the dominant religion and brings associated culture, for example, in social hierarchy and gender roles.

These cultural features contribute to commonalities in school curricula. Most obvious is that Arabic is a core subject, though supplemented by English as an international language. Islamic studies are also core subjects for most students, at least in government schools. And cultural features also shape the tone of educational delivery. Thus, as observed by Kirdar (2017, p. 1), school curricula across much of the region transmit 'prepackaged

DOI: 10.4324/9781003317593-3

bodies of knowledge that reinforce discipline' but, she felt, 'bear little need to relate to either students' concerns and interests or national needs' (see also Rohde & Alayan, 2012, p. 4).

Social, economic and political diversities

Despite these commonalities, within the region are major social, economic and political diversities. First, taking the nation-state as a unit and noting population, Iraq has 40.6 million people while Bahrain has only 1.7 million (Table 3.1). By contrast, Bahrain is by far the most densely populated with 2,180 people per square kilometre, while Oman has just 22. Population size and density are among significant factors for entrepreneurs considering offer of services that accompany or provide alternatives to public education systems. Even more important to entrepreneurs is wealth. Whereas Qatar's per capita GDP was US$70,700, Yemen's was US$900. Household incomes clearly shape families' ability to afford private educational services and therefore underpin tutoring in prosperous societies, but tutoring may also be evident in low-income societies because state budgets for education are constrained and families decide to stretch their own resources in order to bridge gaps.

Table 3.1 Features of Middle East Countries

Country	Area (km^2)	Population (2020, million)	Density (per km^2)	Per capita GDP (2018, US$)	Official language(s)
Bahrain	780	1.7	2,180	25,900	Arabic
Iraq	438,317	40.6	93	5,900	Arabic, Kurdish
Jordan	92,300	10.2	110	4,300	Arabic
Kuwait	17,820	4.3	241	30,800	Arabic
Lebanon	10,452	6.8	645	9,300	Arabic
Oman	212,460	4.6	22	19,300	Arabic
Palestine	6,220	4.8	772	3,600	Arabic
Qatar	11,437	2.4	210	70,700	Arabic
Saudi Arabia	2,149,690	34.7	16	23,600	Arabic
Syria	185,180	21.4	116	n.a.	Arabic
United Arab Emirates	82,880	9.2	111	40,700	Arabic
Yemen	527,970	29.7	56	900	Arabic

Sources: Various, including https://en.wikipedia.org/wiki/Middle_East; https://en.wikipedia.org/wiki/List_of_Middle_Eastern_countries_by_population, accessed 1 March 2020.

Note: n.a. = not available.

18 *Middle East contexts*

Also of major contextual importance are political factors. Abdel-Moneim (2016, pp. 52–54), with a broader focus on the MENA region, distinguished between the 'rentier states' and the 'socialist republics'. Most prominent among the former were the high-income GCC countries, in which the ruling elites had substantial resources to distribute to their populations. In contrast were the socialist republics, most obviously Egypt and others that since the early 1950s had been influenced by the Arab socialist project led by Egyptian President Gamal Abdel Nasser. In 1958, Syria integrated with Egypt in the United Arab Republic (which included the Palestinian Gaza Strip) until separation again in 1961 following which it nevertheless retained close ties. Other socialist republics have included Algeria, Tunisia, Sudan and Yemen (Richards & Waterbury, 2008, p. 291). However, classifications cannot be clear-cut. Thus, although many non-GCC countries in the Levant do not rely on a single natural resource, they receive substantial remittances from workers in rentier states along with foreign aid of various kinds. Furthermore, although Iraq has oil resources, its development track from the early 1960s was 'clearly influenced by the socialist model in terms of domestic and social policies as well as regional and international politics' (Abdel-Moneim, 2016, p. 53).

These political and related economic and social frameworks have various strands of relevance for education, including private tutoring. Prior to the oil boom of 1960s and 1970s, Kuwait, Qatar, Bahrain and the Emirates that now comprise the UAE had low incomes, were thinly populated, and had very limited educational provision. In Qatar, for example, before the start of modern schooling in the 1950s, the only form of education was the traditional provision by one teacher (*Mutawa*) to groups of girls or boys (*al Kuttab*) and mainly focused on memorisation of the Quran with basic Arabic orthography and simple arithmetic (Al-Maadheed, 2017, p. 180). In 1952, Qatar had just one elementary school (for boys); yet by 1980, it had 141 schools (71 for boys and 70 for girls). Kuwait had a longer history of schooling in the accepted contemporary mode, with the first institution having been established in 1911 (Al Sharekh, 2017, p. 138); but provision remained very limited prior to independence in 1961 and the creation of a Ministry of Education the following year. Similarly, prior to 1970 Oman had 'no comprehensive educational system' (Al Ghanboosi, 2017, p. 157), and in that year had only 16 schools. However, the numbers expanded dramatically to 207 schools in 1975, to 588 in 1985, and then to 953 in 1995. Comparable patterns were evident elsewhere in what are now the GCC countries, stimulated by resources from oil and the visions of their respective governments. Yet while oil provided financial resources, personnel to operate the schools had to be recruited from elsewhere. Egypt was a major source, supplemented by neighbours including Lebanon, Jordan,

Syria and Palestine (Ridge et al., 2017). The teachers and administrators brought with them their accustomed approaches, including those concerning private tutoring.

Also pertinent are the severe disruptions experienced by Iraq, Lebanon, Syria and Yemen from civil war or other armed conflict; and Palestine has much ongoing ambiguity about its relationship with Israel in conjunction with sharp political differences within and between the West Bank and the Gaza Strip. These conflicts have damaged national economies and have consumed considerable government resources, with resulting restrictions on finance available for schooling. Yemen is the poorest country among the 12 considered in this study, in part because of many decades of civil war. Syria's economy has also been severely damaged; and within Syria, the regimes that dominate different parts of the country have contrasting views of schooling (Fayek, 2017). Lebanon also has much internal diversity. It is governed on a system of 'consociation', which is a political method for power-sharing in the mosaic of religious sectarian and other communities; and this system has implications for education as well as for other domains (Abouchedid & Bou Zeid, 2017; Mahfouz, 2021).

Returning to the GCC countries, a further contextual feature concerns the scale and composition of non-national (expatriate) populations. All GCC countries have considerable numbers of non-nationals, with many employees for manual labour at one end of social class and for high-level management at the other end. Most striking are Qatar and the UAE, where in both cases non-nationals comprise 87% of the total populations; and among the seven UAE emirates, non-nationals comprise 91% in Dubai (Table 3.2). Within the UAE as a whole, the largest groups are Indian (27% of the total population), Pakistani (13%), Filipino (6%) and Egyptian (4%); but the further 39% of the total population comprises a very wide range, including East Asians, West Europeans, North Americans, and Sub-Saharan Africans. Some non-nationals leave their families in their own countries, but others bring their families including school-aged children. Among pertinent implications for the present study is that the non-national families also bring their own cultural attitudes towards private tutoring.

Roles of the state

The 12 countries addressed by this study show some similarities but also striking diversity in both official and de facto roles of the state in education. At the overarching level, all governments proclaim adherence to the principle that education is a human right that they have a duty to actualise and protect in line with the Universal Declaration of Human Rights (United Nations, 1948) and the Convention on the Rights of the Child (United

20 Middle East contexts

Table 3.2 National and Non-national Populations, GCC Countries

	Population (million)	Population national (%)	Population non-national (%)
Bahrain	1.7	45	55
Kuwait	4.3	30	70
Oman	4.6	56	44
Qatar	2.4	13	87
Saudi Arabia	34.7	62	38
United Arab Emirates	9.2	13	87
Dubai	3.3	9	91
Abu Dhabi	3.2	19	81
Sharjah	1.5	12	88
Ajman	0.5	n.a.	n.a.
Ras al-Khaimah	0.4	24	76
Fujairah	0.2	39	61
Umm al-Quwain	0.1	n.a.	n.a.

Sources: *https://gulfmigration.org/gcc-total-population-and-percentage-of-nationals-and-non-nationals-in-gcc-countries-national-statistics-2017–2018-with-numbers/*; *https://en.wikipedia.org/wiki/Middle_East*, *https://gulfmigration.org/uae-population-estimates-by-nationality-emirati-non-emirati-and-sex-last-available-estimates-as-of-march-2018/* accessed 6 February 2021.

Notes: Statistics are for most recent year, in most cases 2018. n.a. = not available.

Nations, 1989). However, the details of enactment vary; and while the United Nations resolutions envisage full and equal access to public schools, they do not pre-empt the existence of private schools. Private tutoring was not a part of the agenda in 1948, so is absent from consideration in the Universal Declaration even though it may be a major instrument for creating and maintaining social inequalities (Bray & Kwo, 2013). It was also absent from the Convention on the Rights of the Child; and it has no specific place in the related Abidjan Principles on the Right to Education (Abidjan Principles, 2019; Adamson et al., 2021). Governments then determine their own approaches not only to the overall roles of the state in education but also to private tutoring and the issues that it raises.

Among the 12 countries considered in this study, the GCC countries may again be considered as one group and the other six countries as another group. Yet again much diversity in the official and de facto roles of the state is evident within each group.

Concerning the GCC countries, it is useful to commence with Saudi Arabia, where the authorities have chosen far-reaching roles for the state. Public expenditures on education rose in the 1970s and 1980s, and then stabilised at a high level. In 2006, only Costa Rica, Lesotho and Oman were reported to devote higher percentages of their budgets to public education (Henry & Springborg, 2010, p. 230). Saudi Arabia's 2006 figure represented 6.8% of

GDP, contrasting with 4.1% as the average for upper-middle-income countries and 5.4% for high-income countries, and was exceeded by only a handful of other countries including Denmark, Norway, Israel and Tunisia. Later figures indicated even higher expenditures. Aldaghishy (2019, p. 116) cited official indications that in 2009 education consumed 26.0% of the government budget and 9.5% of GDP.

Despite these expenditures, according to Aldaghishy (2019, p. 9), the quality of much education in Saudi Arabia was considered mediocre, especially when viewed from the perspective of economics and employment; and although various measures were introduced to improve cost-effectiveness, they were not perceived to have much impact. In 2016, for example, the average teacher to pupil ratio was 1:9, compared with 1:15 in what was described as the regional standard and 1:25 in the international standard (but much greater in many low-income countries); yet the country had performed among the lowest in the international benchmarking TIMSS of 2003, 2007, 2011 and 2015 (Aldaghishy, 2019, p. 99).[1] Private tutoring, which might have boosted performance, was frowned upon; but the government did allow public schools to provide remunerated supplementary services in 'centres for educational services' for students seeking either remedial support or enrichment (Al-Husseini, 2012; Saudi Arabia, 2015).

Patterns in Dubai, which has the largest population of the UAE's seven Emirates, provide a contrast. Compared with Saudi Arabia, Dubai has even greater per capita GDP and thus available resources; but for the education of non-national populations, which comprise 91% of the total, the state has historically played a minimal role. Public schools are designated to serve Emiratis rather than non-nationals, and in 2019 served only 10% of the total student population (Al Ali et al., 2019, p. 1). Prior to the mid-2000s, neither the national authorities nor the Dubai government had a firm grasp on patterns in the private sector, and in 2006 they recognised a lack of even basic data on teachers, students, transition rates and infrastructure (Thacker & Cuadra, 2014, p. 22). In that year, the Knowledge and Human Development Authority (KHDA) was established to undertake oversight of the private sector, and by stages it became a well-organised and powerful institution for monitoring and regulation. However, even with this oversight the bulk of Dubai's schooling remained unsupported by the government. As such, the model contrasted sharply with that in Saudi Arabia, where even the private-oriented body created in 2008 to strengthen market forces in education, Tatweer Education Holding Company, was operated with public funding (Aldaghishy, 2019, p. 82). Like their counterparts in Saudi Arabia, the Dubai government is ambivalent about private tutoring. In 2012, the KHDA considered questions about licensing and accompanying regulations for private tutoring enterprises (Shabbanari, 2012), but decided largely to continue with a laissez-faire approach (KHDA, 2013).

Patterns in Qatar provide a third variation. Per capita incomes in Qatar are even greater than those in Dubai, and the authorities, like their counterparts in Saudi Arabia, have made available considerable resources for education. Again, however, they have been disappointed by qualitative performance as demonstrated by international benchmarks, in this case, the Programme for International Student Assessment (PISA) managed by the Organisation for Economic Co-operation and Development (OECD) (Al-Maadheed, 2017, p. 193).

Within Qatar, as in Dubai, private schools dominate. In 2017/18, they accommodated 61.8% of students, compared with 38.2% in public schools (Qatar, 2020, p. xi). Within the private sector are three types: international schools (locally known as English private schools), community schools offering curricula from other countries such as India, France, Germany and Japan, and private Arabic schools that stress the Arabic language and Islamic studies (Al-Maadheed, 2017, pp. 185–186). In an effort to shake up the public schools, a reform initiated in 2001 transformed them into Independent Schools comparable to the Charter Schools in the USA, and English to some extent displaced Arabic as the medium of instruction. This shift caused many reverberations and was reversed in 2016 (Abdel-Moneim, 2020). The language policy had the unintended consequence of expanding demand for private tutoring both to enhance competence in English and to maintain competence in Arabic. Despite the low achievement of students in public schools and the fact that private schools are the majority, private tutoring is officially prohibited though in practice has been widespread.

Contrasting with the aforementioned prosperous GCC countries are the others in which economic stringency combines with political forces to create very different circumstances. Thus, commencing with Lebanon, the 18 officially recognised sectarian communities living under the national umbrella all have their own education systems; and, as remarked by Mahfouz (2021, p. 109), Lebanon 'has never had a state-led development system'. During and after the 1975–1990 civil war, the Ministry of Education attempted to cultivate social unity through a cohesive curriculum and national assessments for both private and public schools, and opened more public schools. However, economic and political forces brought continued challenges. In 2005, public expenditures on education represented 2.6% of GDP, but by 2011, they had declined to 1.6% (Soueid et al., 2014, p. 4). Private expenditures formed 4.7% of GDP in 2011, making a total of 7.3% in that year. Thus, private expenditures were by far the dominant domain.

Mahfouz (2021, p. 112) added remarks about the impact of neoliberalism in Lebanon as the 2010s progressed. Private schools comprised over half the total, and an average of five public schools per year closed while new private schools (especially for-profit ones) were opened. Neoliberalism, Mahfouz remarked (p. 112), 'contributed to the collapse of public education . . . by surfacing tensions between the right to education and freedom of education'. Private tutoring flourished alongside schooling, and many families found that they were 'paying for two schools' (Al-Haj, 2018).

Further contrasts may be made with Syria and Yemen, both of which have suffered from internal conflict and weak governments (Samier, 2021). Prior to Syria's 2011 protests that escalated into civil war, the country is reported to have had 'a good basic education system with good reputation, controlled and run by the state' (Fayek, 2017, p. 98). The subsequent conflict led to the decline and decimation. Areas remaining under control of the regime led by President Bashar Al-Assad sought to maintain schooling operations but had to do so in the face of much physical damage to facilities and emotional damage to students, parents and teachers. Similar remarks applied both to areas under rebel control and to those under the control of the Islamic State of Iraq and Syria (ISIS). Even in the areas served by the Al-Assad government, by 2016 over a quarter of the teachers had left their posts. Many teachers, from all regions, had left the country altogether. In the ISIS-controlled area, schooling was radically reoriented to 'shape the minds of children according to [the regime's] extreme interpretation of Islam' (Fayek, 2017, p. 107). All teachers and administrative staff were forced to attend Sharia courses and threatened with physical punishment for violations of the ISIS educational policy. Under such circumstances, private tutoring may have served some Syrian families as a default replacement and supplement for schooling, but in the ISIS-controlled areas in at least some instances it met harsh penalties.[2]

Parallels in Yemen included the diversion of budgetary and human resources from education to the military, and related demands of the warring factions (Samier, 2021). In the mid-2010s, 80% of the population needed assistance to meet essential needs of food, water, healthcare and shelter, and for protecting their basic rights including education (Al-Hussaini & Modhesh, 2017, p. 248). About 10% of the population had been displaced, and armed conflict had resulted in both the loss of male breadwinners for many families and notable increase in recruiting children as soldiers. The state remained the dominant supplier of schooling, with the private sector offering only 4.7% of enrolments in 2012/13, and government expenditures on education increased from 13% of the total budget in 2008 to 19% in 2011 (Al-Hussaini & Modhesh, 2017, p. 252). However, these proportions were of a modest overall budget because of economic stringency. In these circumstances, private tutoring may for some families have been a default strategy to bridge gaps (*New Arab*, 2018; Al-Sabahi, 2021), though most were unable to afford it.

In summary, considerable diversity exists in both the official and the de facto roles of the state concerning education in the 12 countries covered by this study. The aforementioned remarks on Saudi Arabia, Dubai and Qatar could be elaborated in the GCC context with observations about the other UAE emirates and about Bahrain, Kuwait and Oman. Likewise, in the other group, the remarks about Lebanon, Syria and Yemen could be elaborated with observations about Iraq, Jordan and Palestine. The implications of these contextual factors will become further evident in the following remarks that turn more specifically to the scale and nature of shadow education, to its educational and social impact, and to policy implications.

Notes

1 Saudi Arabia also performed poorly in the 2019 TIMSS survey as recorded by the TIMSS and PIRLS Databases, Boston College (https://timssandpirls.bc.edu).
2 In 2015, for example, the Syrian press reported ISIS whipping of teachers who had provided private tutoring and of fathers of female students who had received private tutoring (Arabic Sky News, 2015).

References

Abdel-Moneim, Mohamed Alaa (2016): *A Political Economy of Arab Education: Policies and Comparative Perspectives*. London: Routledge.

Abdel-Moneim, Mohamed Alaa (2020): 'Between Global and National Prescriptions for Educational Administration: The Rocky Road of Neoliberal Education Reform in Qatar'. *International Journal of Educational Development*, Vol.74, pp. 1–16.

Abidjan Principles (2019): *Abidjan Principles on the Right to Education*. www.abidjanprinciples.org/

Abouchedid, Kamal & Bou Zeid, Maria (2017): 'Lebanon: Legacy of the Past and Present Challenges', in Kirdar, Serra (ed.), *Education in the Arab World*. London: Bloomsbury, pp. 59–84.

Adamson, Frank; Aubry, Sylvain; de Koning, Mireille & Dorsi, Delphine (eds.) (2021): *Realizing the Abidjan Principles on the Right to Education: Human Rights, Public Education, and the Role of Private Actors in Education*. Cheltenham: Edward Elgar.

Al Ali, Mariam; Mazheruddin, Mohammed; Naismith, Luke & Testa, Simon (2019): *Dubai, UAE*. Boston: TIMSS & PIRLS International Study Center, Boston College. https://timssandpirls.bc.edu/timss2019/encyclopedia/pdf/Dubai%20UAE.pdf

Aldaghishy, Thamir (2019): *The Influence of the Global Education Reform Movement on Saudi Arabia's Education Policy Reforms: A Qualitative Study*. PhD dissertation, St Louis University.

Al Ghanboosi, Salim Saleem (2017): 'Oman: An Overview', in Kirdar, Serra (ed.), *Education in the Arab World*. London: Bloomsbury, pp. 157–178.

Al-Haj, Faten (2018): 'Private Tutoring Institutes: A Censorship-Free Business – Lebanese are Paying for Two Schools'. *Al-Akhbar*, 1 April. https://al-akhbar.com/Education/247538 [in Arabic]

Al-Hussaini, Khalil & Modhesh, Abdullah (2017): 'Yemen: A Historical and Contemporary Overview', in Kirdar, Serra (ed.), *Education in the Arab World*. London: Bloomsbury, pp. 243–260.

Al-Husseini, Shayaa bin Abdulaziz (2012): 'Centres for Educational Services to Limit Private Tutoring in Saudi Arabia'. Document Presented at the Symposium on 'Private Tutoring in the Arab States: Problems and Solutions'. Cairo: League of Arab States. [in Arabic]

Al-Maadheed, Fatma (2017): 'Qatar: Past, Present and Prospects for Education', in Kirdar, Serra (ed.), *Education in the Arab World*. London: Bloomsbury, pp. 179–196.

Al-Sabahi, Mounir Mohammed (2021): *The Strategic Risks of the Salary Cut Crisis in Education in Yemen: Field Research Involving 336 Educators and Academics in Eight Governorates*. Aden: Arabia Felix Center for Studies. المخاطر الاستراتيجية لأزمة انقطاع المرتبات على التعليم في اليمن

Al Sharekh, Alanoud (2017): 'Kuwait: Education and Development', in Kirdar, Serra (ed.), *Education in the Arab World*. London: Bloomsbury, pp. 138–156.

Bray, Mark & Kwo, Ora (2013): 'Behind the Façade of Fee-Free Education: Shadow Education and Its Implications for Social Justice'. *Oxford Review of Education*, Vol.39, No.4, pp. 480–497.

Fayek, Rasha (2017): 'Syria: Educational Decline and Decimation', in Kirdar, Serra (ed.), *Education in the Arab World*. London: Bloomsbury, pp. 98–114.

Henry, Clement Moore & Springborg, Robert (2010): *Globalization and the Politics of Development in the Middle East* (second edition). Cambridge: Cambridge University Press.

KHDA [Knowledge & Human Development Authority] (2013): *Supplementary Private Tutoring in Dubai* (Unpublished report). Dubai: KHDA.

Kirdar, Serra (2017): 'Introduction – Regional Overview', in Kirdar, Serra (ed.), *Education in the Arab World*. London: Bloomsbury, pp. 1–17.

Mahfouz, Julia (2021): 'Neoliberalism – The Straw That Broke the Back of Lebanon's Education System', in Arar, Khalid; Örücü, Deniz & Wilkinson, Jane (eds.), *Neoliberalism and Education Systems in Conflict: Exploring Challenges Across the Globe*. London: Routledge, pp. 107–117.

New Arab (2018): 'Using WhatsApp for Tutoring in Yemen', 24 February. دروس عبر "واتساب" في اليمن [in Arabic]

Ofori-Attah, Kwabena Dei (2008): *Going to School in the Middle East and North Africa*. Westport: Greenwood Press.

Qatar, Ministry of Education and Higher Education (2020): *Annual Statistics of Education in the State of Qatar 2017–2018*. Doha: Ministry of Education and Higher Education.

Richards, Alan & Waterbury, John (2008): *A Political Economy of the Middle East* (third edition). Boulder: Westview Press.

Ridge, Natasha; Soha, Shami & Kippels, Susan (2017): 'Arab Migrant Teachers in the United Arab Emirates and Qatar: Challenges and Opportunities', in Babar, Zahra (ed.), *Arab Migrant Communities in the GCC*. Oxford: Oxford University Press, pp. 39–63.

Rohde, Achim & Alayan, Samira (2012): 'Introduction', in Alayan, Samira; Rohde, Achim & Dhouib, Sarhan (eds.), *The Politics of Education Reform in the Middle East: Self and Other in Textbooks and Curricula*. New York: Berghahn Books, pp. 1–14.

Samier, Eugenie A. (2021): 'Educational Administration Challenges in the Destabilised and Disintegrating States of Syria and Yemen: The Intersectionality of Violence, Culture, Ideology, Class/Status Group and Postcoloniality', in Arar, Khalid; Örücü, Deniz & Wilkinson, Jane (eds.), *Neoliberalism and Education Systems in Conflict: Exploring Challenges across the Globe*. London: Routledge, pp. 135–150.

Saudi Arabia, Ministry of Education (2015): *Circular to All Male Students' Schools (in Relation to Establishing Centres for Educational Services in the Second Semester of the Academic Year 1436–1437 Hijri). No. 37183709, 22/01/1437 Hijri*. Riyadh: Ministry of Education. [in Arabic] [Parallel Circulars Sent on a Regular Basis for Each Semester, and Also to Female Students' Schools]

Shabbanari, Shafaat (2012): 'KHDA to Target Private Tutors in Dubai: KHDA Working on Regulations to Curb Flourishing Tutorial Business'. *GulfNews*, 21 June. https://gulfnews.com/uae/education/khda-to-target-private-tutors-in-dubai-1.1038307

Soueid, Mazen; Ghanem, Stephanie; Hariri, Ziad; Yamout, Nadine & Nehme, Rita (2014): *Analysis of Lebanon's Education Sector*. Beirut: Market & Economic Research Division, BankMed. www.bankmed.com.lb/BOMedia/subservices/categories/News/20150515170635891.pdf

Thacker, Simon & Cuadra, Ernesto (2014): *The Road Traveled: Dubai's Journey Towards Improving Private Education – A World Bank Review*. Washington: The World Bank.

United Nations (1948): *Universal Declaration of Human Rights*. New York: United Nations. www.ohchr.org/EN/UDHR/Documents/UDHR_Translations/eng.pdf

United Nations (1989): *Convention on the Rights of the Child*. New York: United Nations. www.ohchr.org/en/professionalinterest/pages/crc.aspx

4 Scale and nature of shadow education

Enrolment rates

As shown in Box 4.1, the phenomenon of private tutoring is not new in the Middle East region but has considerably expanded in recent decades. A 2012 overview of Arab states stated that shadow education in a subregion, including Bahrain, Kuwait, Lebanon, Iraq, Oman and the UAE, 'had spread in all educational stages from elementary to higher studies' (League of Arab States, 2012, p. 8). It estimated that 50% of students in these countries had received private tutoring during their primary or secondary schooling, and that this percentage might reach to 85% in the final grade.

> **Box 4.1 A Long-standing Issue**
>
> Writing about Kuwait, Hussein (1987) reported that even in the mid-1960s some of the students in the school where he taught received private lessons at home. Indeed, the Ministry of Education had issued a circular on the matter as early as 1962 (Kuwait, 1962). By the mid-1980s, Hussein wrote (p. 91), the problem was 'felt everywhere':
>
>> It affects students in their schools, it reaches into their homes, and now there are so-called institutes in all areas of Kuwait which are directed by teachers from the end of school until midnight. They are charging [considerable fees] for a 45-minute lesson in secondary school mathematics. The problem is also spreading to intermediate (Grades 4–7) and even primary students.
>
> Other reports from the same era and earlier, such as those by Al-Khatib (1982) in Jordan and by Jamal (1965) in Saudi Arabia, pointed in a similar direction.

DOI: 10.4324/9781003317593-4

Table 4.1 elaborates with country-by-country snapshots. Some studies had limited samples and less rigour than might have been desired, but are nevertheless useful. Table 4.2 supplements with TIMSS data for 2015 and 2019 that were collected with more rigorous sampling.[1] They only refer to Grade 8, however, and the time perspective is limited by the

Table 4.1 Scale of Shadow Education in Middle East Countries

Bahrain	Among 290 students surveyed by Albuhi and Alsadah (1994) in 28 schools, 69% were receiving tutoring. Within the sample, 84% of primary, 58% of intermediate, and 65% of secondary students were receiving tutoring. Students in private schools received more tutoring than counterparts in public schools.
	Enrolment rates evidently remained high. For example, Abbas, Nawal (2020) quoted a teacher who referred to 'unprecedented attendance in private tutoring', especially for secondary students; and another teacher who provided tutoring described a 'super busy schedule from the moment I leave school until midnight'.
	Further data from TIMSS in 2015 and 2019 are presented in Table 4.2
Iraq	Private tutoring emerged visibly when economic crisis allied to the 1980–1988 Iraq–Iran war undermined teachers' salaries (Iraq, 2012). By the 1990s, tutoring had become a norm in the context of perceived poor-quality public schooling (Shadbash & Albakaa, 2017, p. 23).
	A 1996 Al-Qadisiyah University study examined the experiences of 514 veterinary and education students when they were in Grades 6–12 (Jassem & Kazem, 2001). The researchers found that 21% of males and 24% of females had received tutoring in at least one subject. English and mathematics were the most popular subjects.
	A 2019/20 random survey of 120 Grade 11 students in four high schools found that 70% of males and 72% of females were receiving private tutoring (Kamil, 2021, p. 412).
Jordan	A 1992/93 survey of 718 upper secondary science students, comprising 9% of the total in 27 schools of Greater Amman, focused on mathematics (Al-Ahmad, 1994). It found that 51% were receiving private tutoring in the subject.
	In a 2004/05 survey, 54% of 1,037 parents from all main regions indicated that their children had received tutoring during primary and/or secondary schooling (Alhabashna & Alnaemi, 2012). Grade 11 students had the highest enrolment rates (54%), followed by Grade 10 (12%). They received tutoring mainly in mathematics (33%), English (31%), biology (13%), and Arabic (11%). Enrolment rates were higher for males than for females except in Grade 1.
	Alhawarin and Karaki (2012, p. 131), citing data from the 2010 Jordan Labor Market Panel Survey, indicated that about 15% of households spent money on private tutoring, mainly to prepare their children for the Higher Secondary Education Examination.
	Table 4.2 presents further data from TIMSS in 2015 and 2019.

Kuwait	A 1987 survey of 934 students in Grades 5–12 who were being tutored in at least one subject found that 77% were receiving tutoring in mathematics, 55% in physics, 45% in chemistry, 12% in biology, 15% in English, 6% in Arabic, and 2% in religion (Hussein, 1987, p. 94). In 2009, researchers surveyed 785 students and 274 parents at different secondary schools of five cities (Al-Salhi et al., 2009). Among the students, 69% said that they were receiving tutoring, but 86% of parents said that their children were receiving it. A random sample of 40 students in Grades 11–12 in four schools of one district found that 62.5% were receiving private tutoring (Al-Mari & Al-Khamees, 2013). A random 1% sample of parents throughout the country found that 44% of children across all grades were receiving tutoring (Al-Shati & Sabti, 2012). Table 4.2 presents further data from TIMSS in 2015 and 2019.
Lebanon	Dabaga (2014, p. 135) indicated that many families wanted their children to join English-medium universities in Lebanon or abroad. They received tutoring, especially in English, for high-stakes examinations. The phenomenon is also remarked upon by many press commentaries (e.g. Abdulkareem, 2015; Alawya, 2017; Al-Haj, 2018; Farhat, 2014). Table 4.2 presents further data from TIMSS in 2015 and 2019.
Oman	A 2012 report noted significant expansion of private tutoring, especially among Grades 10 and 11 students in Muscat, in the context of growing household incomes and expatriate teachers' desires to supplement their salaries (Oman, 2012). Male students received more tutoring than females because of the lack of female tutors and long-standing traditions that restricted female students from visiting tutors in their homes and from using public transport. Table 4.2 presents further data from TIMSS in 2019.
Palestine	A 2016 survey of 100 female students in Grades 10–12 at different schools in the Gaza Strip found that 69% received tutoring (Askr & Al-Shrehi, 2016). Among them, 85% received tutoring in English, 69% in mathematics, 19% in physics, 16% in chemistry, and 11% in Arabic. A 2018 survey of 122 female Grade 11 students in one East Jerusalem school found that 25% of arts stream students received tutoring, mainly in English (57%) and Arabic (23%) (Al-Atrash, 2018). In the science stream, 38% of students received tutoring, mainly in English (23%), physics (20%) and mathematics (8%).

(*Continued*)

30 Scale and nature of shadow education

Table 4.1 (Continued)

Qatar	Brewer et al. (2007, p. 31), citing official sources, indicated that in 1995/96, about a third of students in public schools received private lessons. The 2012 PISA survey reported that 59% of 15-year-olds were receiving supplementary tutoring, though the responses could include unpaid as well as paid tutoring (Entrich, 2021). A 2015 national survey secured information from 1,803 students in 38 secondary schools (Alemadi et al., 2016, p. 22). Across all school types, 46% of Qatari and 28% of expatriate students received private tutoring. In international schools, respective figures were 55% and 39%. A 2018 follow-up survey collected data from 1,639 students in 34 schools (Sellami, 2019, p. 12). Proportions of students receiving tutoring were 38% in Grade 8, 40% in Grade 9, 35% in Grade 11 and 56% in Grade 12. In government schools, the proportion was 45%, and in international schools it was 34%. Table 4.2 presents further data from TIMSS in 2015 and 2019.
Saudi Arabia	A 2013 survey of 300 randomly selected students in 30 Jeddah girls' secondary schools found that, discarding the 12% who did not respond to the question, 97% of students were receiving tutoring and only 3% were not (Taeb & Falmbaan, 2013). Table 4.2 presents further data from TIMSS in 2015 and 2019.
Syria	Ghanem et al. (2021) surveyed 377 parents of lower-secondary students in Lattakia city. Almost all (94.5%) reported that their children received private tutoring in at least three subjects. Other authors have also highlighted the phenomenon, albeit without statistical data (see, e.g. Al-Marashli, 2012; Al-Yousifi, 2015; Enab Baladi, 2019; Shamra, 2020). It is driven especially by teachers' low salaries.
United Arab Emirates	A 1995/96 survey of 2,975 Emirati intermediate and secondary school students across the country found that 90% were receiving tutoring (Bouklah & Al-Khayal, 1997). A 2011 study of 180 Emirati students in the foundation year at UAE University found that 66% had received tutoring during their last year of schooling (Farah, 2011, p. 2). A 2012/13 Dubai survey of students in Grades 9 and 12 indicated that 49% had received tutoring in the past year (KHDA, 2013, p. 17). In Indian-curriculum schools, 70% had received tutoring, while in schools following Ministry of Education, US and UK curricula, the proportion was 38%. Among Arab expatriate children (Bahrain, Egypt, Jordan, Palestine, Qatar, Saudi Arabia and Syria), an average of 31% had received private tutoring. Grade 12 proportions (63%) were greater than Grade 9 (37%). The 2012 PISA survey reported that 54.0% of 15-year-olds were receiving supplementary tutoring, though the responses could include unpaid as well as paid tutoring (Entrich, 2021).

	A study by the Abu Dhabi Education Council (cited by Rocha & Hamed, 2018, p. 10), which surveyed 57,000 parents of public and private school students in the Abu Dhabi Emirate, indicated that 18.1% of students received private tutoring in Arabic. In addition, 17.9% of parents said that their children received tutoring in English, 19.7% in mathematics and 16.2% in science. A 2017/18 national study of 3,929 parents of students in Grades 5, 9, 10 and 12 indicated that 27% of students were receiving tutoring (Rocha & Hamed, 2018, p. 22). Proportions were higher among Emiratis (32%) than non-Emiratis (21%). Table 4.2 presents further data from TIMSS in 2015 and 2019.
Yemen	The education system has been much damaged by civil war and associated economic crisis. Press remarks (e.g. *New Arab*, 2018) and academic studies (e.g. Al-Sabahi, 2021) have highlighted absenteeism of teachers from regular classes and a shift to tutoring in person or online to bridge gaps.

fact that TIMSS surveys before 2015 did not collect data on this topic. Among the major messages for the present report is that much more and better research is needed for both updated and more complete pictures. Meanwhile, the collection of snapshots indicates that tutoring has been and remains

- evident in countries of all income categories;
- especially common in senior-secondary schooling as students face terminal examinations, but also evident in primary and junior secondary schooling;
- commonly received by students in both private and public schools;
- accessed in all social classes, but especially in middle classes (who can afford, and aim to retain their status) compared with lower classes (who are economically constrained) and upper classes (who have alternative ways to retain status through finance and social contacts);
- especially demanded in mathematics and languages (particularly English, and also to some extent Arabic), and in physics and chemistry for students in science streams; and
- more common in urban than rural areas.

Elaborating on Table 4.2, the TIMSS data are especially helpful because they show national samples. In addition, Abu Dhabi and Dubai are shown independently as 'benchmarking participants' (Martin et al., 2016). As might be expected, enrolment rates were greater in mathematics than in science. In 2015, for mathematics, they ranged from 57.9% in Kuwait

Table 4.2 Grade 8 Enrolment Rates and Motives in Supplementary Tutoring, TIMSS, 2015 and 2019 (%)

Country		2015			2019		
		Enrolment rate	Among students receiving tutoring, motive was to excel in class	Among students receiving tutoring, motive was to keep up in class	Enrolment rate	Among students receiving tutoring, motive was to excel in class	Among students receiving tutoring, motive was to keep up in class
Bahrain	Mathematics	54.7	65.2	34.8	46.2	67.7	32.3
	Science	48.2	62.6	37.4	37.7	63.4	36.6
Jordan	Mathematics	50.3	80.0	20.0	45.9	76.5	23.5
	Science	44.9	72.0	28.0	38.2	67.3	32.7
Kuwait	Mathematics	57.9	71.8	28.1	54.8	71.5	28.5
	Science	42.9	65.7	34.3	38.3	65.5	34.5
Lebanon	Mathematics	47.1	68.3	31.7	40.2	61.7	38.3
	Science	42.1	53.8	46.2	36.3	49.3	50.7
Oman	Mathematics	n.a.	n.a.	n.a.	39.6	60.4	39.6
	Science	n.a.	n.a.	n.a.	29.9	50.8	49.2
Qatar	Mathematics	44.9	65.0	35.0	35.6	66.0	44.0
	Science	35.9	60.7	39.3	28.2	63.8	36.2
Saudi Arabia	Mathematics	49.5	72.3	27.7	50.2	72.7	27.3
	Science	46.3	68.6	31.4	47.0	72.1	27.7
UAE	Mathematics	38.6	66.6	33.4	35.9	57.9	42.1
	Science	31.5	60.5	39.5	27.7	55.6	44.4
Abu Dhabi	Mathematics	35.2	60.4	39.6	42.2	49.8	50.2
	Science	25.2	54.7	45.3	35.6	43.0	57.0
Dubai	Mathematics	n.a.	n.a.	n.a.	35.5	58.6	41.4
	Science	n.a.	n.a.	n.a.	24.2	67.4	32.6

Source: TIMSS and PIRLS Databases, Boston College https://timssandpirls.bc.edu.

n.a. = not available: Oman did not participate, and Dubai was not a benchmarking participant, in TIMSS 2015.

to 38.6% in the UAE (see also Figure 4.1); and for science they ranged from 48.2% in Bahrain to 31.5% in the UAE. Since Grade 8 was not a significant transition point in these countries, it may be assumed that rates were higher in subsequent grades and particularly the last grade of secondary schooling at the end of which students sat the high-stakes examinations for university entry. The dominant motive indicated by the students was to excel in class rather than to keep up. In most (but not all) countries, reported enrolment rates dropped slightly between 2015 and 2019.

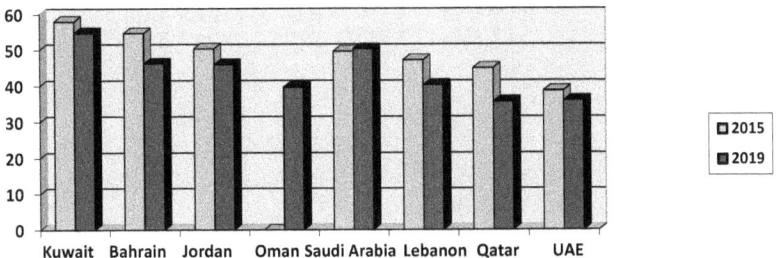

Figure 4.1 Enrolment Rates in Mathematics Supplementary Tutoring, Eight Countries, Grade 8, 2015 and 2019 (%).

Modes and durations

The aforementioned data on enrolment rates conceal many variations. First is in the modes of instruction, which may include one-to-one, small-group, and large-class tutoring. One-to-one tutoring, commonly in the homes of either the tutors or the students but perhaps also in cafés, libraries or other public spaces, is widely considered by both tutors and families the most desirable form because it can be tailored to the students' needs. It is also usually the most costly. Group tutoring can reduce the unit cost, and large-class tutoring can reduce it further.[2] Figure 4.2 shows patterns in the UAE for students in a national survey of Grades 5, 9, 10 and 12 (Rocha & Hamed, 2018, p. 28). In this setting, groups were described as large if they had over five students, implying still modest size compared with classes elsewhere of 30, 40 or even more. The statistics showed that greater proportions of Emirati than non-Emirati students received one-to-one tutoring, probably reflecting the higher incomes of Emirati families.

Also increasingly important as technologies advance, and as both tutors and families become more familiar with this mode, is internet tutoring. It does not seem to have been considered in the 2018 Qatar survey, but has significance even across national borders since tutors and students can even be located not only in different suburbs, cities or rural locations but also in different countries. Internet tutoring permits savings in money and time for travel by the tutor or student, and even other costs may be reduced by outsourcing to locations with lower salary levels (Box 4.2). As shown in Figure 2.1, online tutoring may be live, recorded or mixed; and dual-tutor models may be with humans or artificial intelligence in conjunction with teachers. Tutoring by internet was given a great boost across the world, including in the Middle East, by closure of schools and face-to-face tutorial enterprises during the Covid-19 pandemic that hit in 2020 (Bayoumi, 2020;

34 *Scale and nature of shadow education*

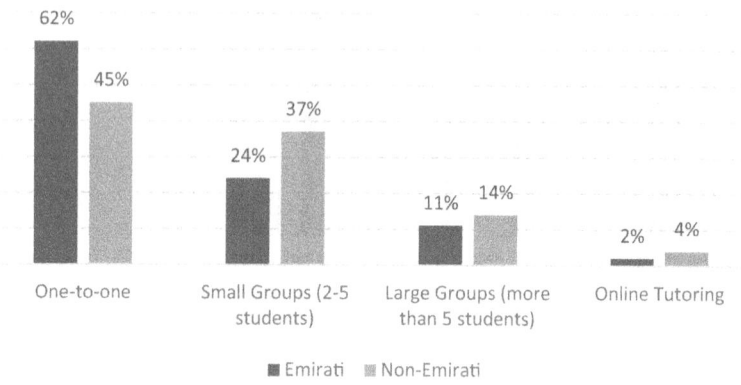

Figure 4.2 Types of Private Tutoring, UAE, 2018.
Source: Rocha and Hamed (2018), p. 28.

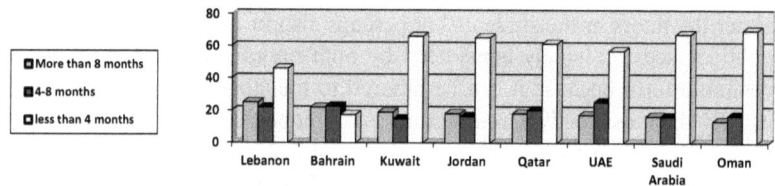

Figure 4.3 Durations of Mathematics Supplementary Tutoring, Eight Countries, Grade 8, 2019 (%). Data refer only to those who received some tutoring. Students with zero hours are excluded.

Source: TIMSS and PIRLS Databases, Boston College *https://timssandpirls.bc.edu*.

Mahmoud & Al-Dhafiri, 2021; Paracha, 2020; Sherman, 2020). With a need to maintain their incomes, and relatively unhampered by bureaucratic traditions and rules, private tutors generally shifted to online work more rapidly than schools; and with schools later catching up, families became even more habituated to online activities.[3]

A further dimension for general mapping concerns the duration of tutoring. Unlike schooling, which can be assumed to be a regular activity occupying students for full days and complete curricula during term-time, tutoring may be irregular and partial. The TIMSS questionnaire cited earlier did ask students about durations of tutoring, and Figure 4.3 shows responses for mathematics tutoring received by Grade 8 students in 2019. The largest proportions, reaching 69.8% in Saudi Arabia, received tutoring for less than

Box 4.2 Harnessing Technology and Transcending National Boundaries

Saudi Arabia hosts a popular internet platform for private tutoring called Noon Academy. Established in 2013, within four years it had attracted over a million secondary students; and after a further four years it claimed to be 'loved by 10+ million students and 100k teachers across 8 countries'.

Noon employs a 'freemium' model, with free initial access and then payment for additional services. Flash cards explain educational content, and exercises permit students to receive scores. Users can then for a fee secure support from private tutors, who respond with instant messages or voice calls and can use the phone or tablet to help students with graphs and other means.

During the initial years, most tutors were in Egypt and provided their services much more cheaply than Saudi tutors. In 2017, for example, whereas Saudi tutors usually charged 180–250 riyals per hour (US$48–66), the platform charged around 50 riyals per hour.

Among keys to the platform's success has been the combination of functionality with social and 'gamification' features. Mohammed Aldhalaan, Noon's co-founder and chief executive officer, explained: 'Our fully interactive and fun platform has been built on the insight that the biggest obstacle to learning isn't comprehension, but rather boredom'.

Business was also much boosted by Covid-19. Within four months of the outbreak, Noon had doubled its userbase by adding three million new students. The next stage of growth was expected to involve schools themselves. Mohammed Aldhalaan planned to 'add functionality that will enable schools around the world to easily utilize the platform to address their specific needs'. This was particularly relevant when students continued to study from home, and was likely to become a permanent feature.

Sources: Paracha (2020); Rahal (2017); *www.noonacademy.com*.

four months in the year, probably in the period leading up to the end-of-year examinations or during the long vacations. By contrast, 25.0% of students in Lebanon received tutoring for more than eight months, which probably meant all the year round. Further detail on such matters is desirable and should be added to research agendas.

Another aspect of duration concerns intensity. Thus, students are likely to receive more hours per day as they approach crucial examinations, and then possible relaxation until the next season. During the intensive seasons, they may receive tutoring before as well as after school, and on weekends and during public holidays. The Qatar 2018 national survey of private tutoring received by students in Grades 8, 9, 10 and 11 showed that 52% of respondents received private tutoring weekly (Sellami, 2019, p. 25). The next highest category (20%) received tutoring during examination periods, while 16% received daily tutoring, 6% monthly tutoring, and 6% 'other'. As might be expected, prices during the examination season were higher than at other seasons – according to one source (Suliman & Alfakki, 2018) typically doubling the ordinary season price to reach 200 riyals (US$55) per hour.

Drivers of demand

In all systems around the world, the fundamental driver of demand for private tutoring is social competition. Since performance in schooling is a principal vehicle for such competition, most tutoring is underpinned by desire to achieve high – or at least adequate – scores in examinations. International research has shown that systems with high-stakes assessments at watershed points are more likely to have strong incidence of private tutoring (Zwier et al., 2020); but even the relatively low-stakes assessments during and at the end of each academic year strongly shape private tutoring because they influence students' peer dynamics and self-esteem, and also teachers' attitudes towards students.

At the same time, distinctions may be made between low-achieving students needing tutoring to keep up with their peers, and high-achieving students wanting to maintain and extend their track records. Table 4.2 indicates that, as reported by the students themselves, high achievement was the dominant motive in most countries presented. This matched the broader picture conveyed by the TIMSS data, and suggests that private tutoring – at least in these subjects and at this grade – is more likely to expand achievement gaps than to narrow them.

Among factors behind these differences are socio-economic disparities. Around the world, students in higher social classes are more likely to receive private tutoring than counterparts in lower social classes (Entrich, 2021; Jansen et al., 2021). This pattern reflects not only the ability of these families to afford the tutoring but also the stronger ambitions in the higher social classes and the students' already-demonstrated accomplishments in initial grades of schooling.

Within the overall numbers, as noted in Table 4.1, there may be differences by subject. In many settings, the subjects in greatest demand are mathematics and languages. In the Middle East, Arabic is certainly important;

but since most students feel that they have adequate competence in Arabic, a stronger demand is for English. Mathematics and languages are core subjects not only in themselves but also as keys to success in other subjects. Physics, chemistry and to some extent biology are in much demand among science-track students, and in general the sciences commonly have higher private-tutoring enrolment rates than the arts because they attract more ambitious students. Subjects in low demand include geography, history and religious studies because they are perceived to be easier and less essential for the demonstration of excellence.

Various qualitative studies shed further light on these matters. In Saudi Arabia, for example, Alotaibi (2014, p. 81) interviewed two groups of six Grade-12 students and, separately, four parents of those students. Alotaibi was particularly interested in tutoring for English. Among the students, the core themes were:

- *Difficulty in the subject.* When asked why they found the subject difficult, most interviewees replied that the teacher 'did not explain the lessons well'. The researcher noted the teacher-dominated environment in which students were passive recipients.
- *Weak teacher performance.* Compounding the problem of difficulty, many teachers were described as weak or heavily burdened. One interviewee reported: 'Our teacher is always exhausted when he comes to our class; he only turns pages in our textbook!' Heavy teaching loads in Saudi schools were said to obstruct careful planning, and required teachers to rush through their lessons. Students then had to turn to tutors to reduce their comprehension deficiencies.
- *Examinations.* One student felt that his teacher deliberately set difficult examinations so that the students would get low marks and then come to that teacher for private tutoring. Another student sought private tutoring to gain some idea of the examination format. The examination-oriented teaching practices in Saudi classrooms were a major determinant of the overall picture.

The parents had related responses, but with their own emphases (Alotaibi, 2014, pp. 81–82):

- *Lack of parental follow-up.* Some parents hired tutors to free themselves from the burden of tracking their children's progress. Parents also felt handicapped by insufficient subject competence, especially in the higher grades.
- *Social pressure.* One parent stated that 'Unfortunately, private tutoring has become a form of social show-off'. Some families, the parent

added, hired tutors only because other families in their social circle did so.
- *Student-related causes.* When some students received tutoring, others took that as the norm and then pressed their parents to hire tutors. Another factor was a weak foundation from intermediate school, perhaps from poor teaching but also from cutting classes. Some students felt that so long as they could find someone to explain the lessons and help them to pass the examinations, they only needed to attend school lessons when required by regulations.
- *School-related causes.* Large classes at school prevented teachers from giving individual attention. That not only diminished performance but also caused parents even to question the utility of schooling. One parent explained that 'if our students are not getting the attention they need at school, there is no point of sending them there. We could just go for private tutoring'. Alongside the teachers' capacities were the inhibitions of the students. One parent explained that his son was unwilling to raise questions in front of many peers, but would do so more readily with a private tutor. Parents also felt that tutoring was more strategic. One interviewee referred to the easy-to-study summaries that his son received from the tutor, resulting in high marks.

The aforementioned remarks can to a large extent be generalised across subjects, levels and countries (see, e.g. Aldami, 2017 in Iraq; Alkandari, 2015 in Kuwait; Hatamleh, 2021 in Jordan; Sellami & Le Trung, 2020 in Qatar). They show a combination of student, school and family factors, and also reflect parental concepts of schooling. Thus, remarking further on the parental approval of easy-to-study summaries, Alotaibi (2014, p. 82) noted that at least some participants in the educational process were willing to tolerate superficial knowledge rather than deep understanding.

Cultural factors may also be important, including those for non-nationals bringing the cultures from their home countries. Patterns in Dubai are instructive, because only a relatively small number of government schools exist to serve national families and the majority of schools are operated privately for non-nationals. The KHDA, which oversees the private schools, has recognised 17 curricular systems, many of which have sub-systems (KHDA, 2021). Among countries from which these curricula are derived, in addition to the UAE Ministry of Education, are France, Germany, India, Iran, Japan, Pakistan, the Philippines, Russia, the UK and the USA. For the present study, employing again the metaphor of the shadow, the question is to what extent 17 curricular systems generate 17 shadows. The answer implied by research in 2012 (KHDA, 2013) was that at least 17 shadows would be generated, in part because of the school curricula and the cultures brought by citizens of the countries from which the curricula were derived. Thus students in Indian-curriculum schools, reflecting the culture of India itself, had much greater enrolment rates in private tutoring than counterparts in American-curriculum schools, for example. Another factor concerned the business model. Some schools charged high fees and offered individualised tutoring when needed as part of the total package, while other schools charged low fees for a minimal package and then expected parents to pay extra for tutoring either within or beyond the school as desired (Bray & Ventura, 2022).

Differences and similarities across genders are also important. Historically, Middle East cultures have tended to favour the formal education of males more than females; and in some parts of the region, this pattern has been carried over to private tutoring.[4] In addition to the fact that some parents especially in lower-income countries may favour education of boys more than girls, particularly when it has to be paid for, tutoring for girls may face practical constraints. Thus, among factors presented, for example, in Oman (Oman, Permanent Mission to the League of Arab States, 2012) and Palestine (Affaneh & El-Ajez, 1999) are that for cultural reasons female students and tutors cannot so easily travel alone for tutoring. With such matters in mind, some tutoring institutes specifically advertise provision of transport for females. With such support, and perhaps changing cultural norms, recent statistics commonly show approximate parity in receipt of tutoring or, in some cases, more females than males. Research data, albeit in many cases with small samples, include the following:

- *Bahrain.* Among 290 students surveyed by Albuhi and Alsadah (1994) in 28 schools, 73% of males were receiving tutoring compared with 64% of females.
- *Iraq.* Among 514 university students asked about their experiences in Grades 6–12, Jassem and Kazem (2001) found that 21% of males and 24% of females had received tutoring in at least one subject. The later random survey of 120 Grade-11 students in four high schools by Kamil (2021) found that 70% of males and 72% of females were receiving private tutoring.
- *Jordan.* Al Farra (2009, pp. 82–83) surveyed 2,346 students in Grades 8, 10 and 12 in government and private schools and in Grade 8 in schools run by the United Nations Relief and Works Agency (UNRWA) to serve Palestinian refugees living in Jordan. She found that 38% of sampled males in the government schools received private tutoring, compared with 52% of females. In the private schools respective proportions were equal at 39%, and in the UNWRA schools they were 28% for males and 46% for females.[5]

40 *Scale and nature of shadow education*

- *Qatar.* A 2012 national survey of students in Grades 8, 9, 11 and 12 by the SESRI at Qatar University showed higher male than female enrolment rates in private tutoring (Mandikiana, 2021). A 2018 repeat of the survey echoed: among surveyed students in the four grades, male enrolment rates were 42% compared with female ones of 38% (Sellami, 2019, p. 12).
- *UAE.* The 2011 study of 180 Emirati students in the foundation year at UAE University who had attended public schools found that 73% of males compared with 60% of females had received tutoring when in Grade 12 (Farah, 2011, p. 3). The later national study by Rocha and Hamed (2018, p. 23) found that among sampled Emirati students, 36% of males were receiving tutoring compared with 30% of females. Among non-Emiratis, respective proportions were 23% and 19%.

Even then, further glosses may be identified. Thus, the Qatar study (Sellami, 2019) indicated that males were more likely to receive daily tutoring while females were more likely to receive it only during the examination periods. Different genders also had different reasons for securing private tutoring (Figure 4.4), with males stressing the advice of friends and the sign of wealth but with females emphasising the issue of teachers not explaining well.

On the further side of gender of tutor, the UAE research by Rocha and Hamed (2018, p. 28) indicated some parental preference, especially for

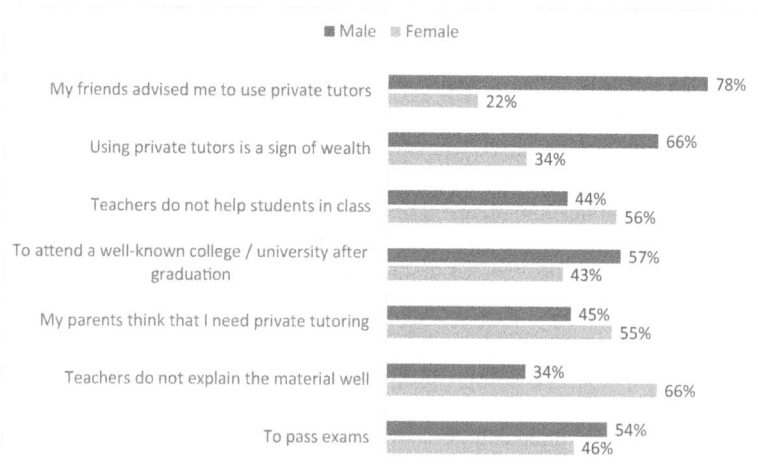

Figure 4.4 Reasons for Securing Private Tutoring, by Gender, Qatar, 2018.
Source: Sellami (2019), p. 22.

Box 4.3 Parental Perspectives on Private Tutoring in Abu Dhabi

In the Emirate of Abu Dhabi, 81% of the population are non-nationals; and as in other parts of the UAE, many non-nationals attend private schools. They usually choose schools following the curricula of their home countries, and the quality can vary. Here are voices from two parents.

M.R. is a Pakistani mother of four children.

> My 15-year old son was falling so far behind in his academics that I was worried he would not pass the Grade 10 exams this June. Moreover, the private school he was enrolled at did not have a physics teacher for months, and the school was not even assessing his knowledge of the subject. Eventually, I was forced to get him started on tuition classes last October.

In addition to annual school fees of 17,000 dirhams (US$4,630), M.R. had to pay 1,000 dirhams on private tutoring per week:

> Each hour-long class was priced at about Dh100, and maths lessons were Dh175 each. The quality of teaching is so bad here that my son even had to take lessons in English. He speaks the language fluently, but his grades are still very weak due to insufficient attention by the teachers.

Another mother is K. Nahar, a Bangladeshi homemaker.

> I do not believe any parent would want their children to attend additional classes after school if the teaching standards were good enough. But my daughter is currently in the ninth grade, and she is simply not able to tackle basic maths problems because teachers are not patient enough to help her.
>
> Eventually I was able to find a graduate student who has generously agreed to lend an hour of his time every day to tutor her in maths and the sciences. Still, I would really prefer it if schools hired better trained teachers so that my daughter would not have to attend extra lessons in the evening.

Source: Zaman and Al Taher (2013).

girls, but still with some leeway. Thus, half of the parents stated that the sex of the tutor was not important, but 30% of boys' parents preferred a male tutor and 17% preferred a female. By contrast, 51% of the girls' parents stated that they would prefer a female tutor and only 5% would prefer a male tutor.

Drivers of supply

The main driver of tutoring supply is the desire by tutors to earn incomes. Thus, teachers supplement the salaries that they receive from schools; university students and other informal workers secure extra pocket money or even full incomes; and companies that run tutorial enterprises seek profits for their owners. Alternatively, some tutors undertake the work as a social contribution, to help students in need (see, e.g. Al-Kafrawi, 2018; Innfrad, 2016). This may be particularly common among retirees, but can also apply to teachers and others.

Tutoring supply has a geographic component (Bray, 2021d). Companies desire sufficient density of population to provide adequate numbers of customers. This leads to an urban bias, with companies often locating their classrooms close to transportation hubs. Teachers, by contrast, are spread throughout rural as well as urban areas; and since commercial companies are less likely to operate face-to-face in rural areas, rural teachers have even greater importance in this respect than their urban counterparts. Within urban areas, companies also pay attention to socioeconomic variations – for example, targeting middle-class suburbs more than working-class ones.

Internet tutoring is less constrained by geographic factors. It does require adequate bandwidth, which is a challenge in parts of Syria and Yemen, for example. One solution there has been to use WhatsApp, which requires only a telephone and a SIM card (*New Arab*, 2018). Elsewhere, internet access is more readily available, and for families able to purchase or otherwise access computers such tutoring, as highlighted in Box 4.2, is unrestricted even by national borders. Thus increasing numbers of tutorial companies operate internationally. While some capitalise on relatively low salaries in such countries as Egypt and India to provide services at modest prices, others capitalise on native speakers of English in such countries as Australia, England and the USA and may provide services at relatively high prices.

The rise of internet tutoring is among the marked shifts over time. Other shifts arise from diversification and responsiveness in the marketplace. Thus, in Saudi Arabia, for example, alongside tutors who focus on examination grades are increasing numbers of 'follow-up tutors' who review everyday classes to help their tutees with basic understanding of subjects and of homework (Aldaghishy, 2021). Others brand themselves as 'foundation tutors', focusing especially on mathematics and reading in the lower grades rather than on the content and examination skills needed for Grade 12.

As might be expected, different subjects, modes and seasons typically have different prices. The array in Qatar has been illustrated by Rao (2017):

- In one of the licensed tutorial centres, yearly fees for the commerce stream were 10,700 riyals (US$2,900) per year for all subjects, while in the science stream, they were 11,700 riyals. The admission fee of 4,500 riyals was separate.
- A private tutor in mathematics for O-level examinations charged 500 riyals per month per subject, holding classes at his home for three hours, five days a week.
- One family with busy working schedules chose to pay a personal tutor to help all children to review their daily studies at school and to receive other individual attention and supervision. The tutor was paid 2,000 riyals per month.
- Another parent with a hectic work schedule sent her five-year-old daughter to a home tutor for two hours per day and four days per week. The tutor charged 300 riyals per month.
- A tutorial centre with a wide range of international curricula charged 5,600 riyals per subject per term, with the term lasting 10 weeks. Each class lasted 1.5 hours.
- A non-national parent reported that her daughter in a Pakistani-curriculum school faced tough competition and 'forced us to send her to the same tutor her friends go to' in order to learn in the same way as them. The tutor charged 1,500 riyals per month for tutoring in three subjects.

In contrast, another mother reported that her daughter attended a school with an American curriculum. The daughter did not receive private tutoring, and to the mother's knowledge the classmates also did not do so. 'These schools do proper coaching and put less pressure on children and parents', she said, while still praising the academic achievements of the school. Nevertheless, this school may have had high fees – with the implication that ultimately the parents were paying an amount comparable to other families.

The next question concerns marketing. Many tutors rely on word of mouth, often with parents of successful pupils passing recommending to other parents. Teachers who provide tutoring may inform their own students (sometimes, placing pressure on them), or may be recommended by their colleagues (see, e.g. Al-Fahdeh, 2019; Hatamleh, 2021). In the

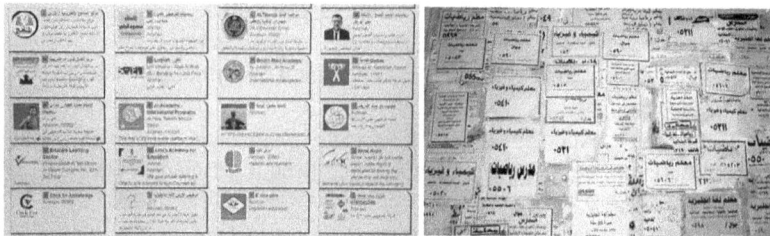

Figure 4.5 Advertising of Tutoring Services, by Internet (Jordan) and Informal Wall Posters (Saudi Arabia).

Sources: Internet screen shot – Mark Bray; informal wall posters – الدروس الخصوصية تغطي الجدران ملصقات (alyaum.com)

UAE, tutorial 'brokers' provide match-making services that link families with tutors.[6] Alternatively, tutors may decide to advertise using formal or informal channels. Figure 4.5 shows multiple advertisements on a Jordanian website and, less formally, home-made slips of paper with telephone numbers on a wall in Saudi Arabia. Tutorial enterprises may advertise via newspapers, magazines and large posters in public spaces.

Further differences in supply of tutoring are evident across individual countries. Particularly in Syria and Yemen, as mentioned, much tutoring has been provided by teachers facing collapse of their salaries in the context of civil war and weak government ability to fund school systems. The teachers have therefore supplied tutoring to bridge income gaps, and some have neglected their mainstream work in ways that make tutoring an essential supplement or even alternative to schooling. Similar patterns were evident in Iraq during the 1980s, when tutoring became an established form of provision, and continued during the 1990s and after.

The high-income countries of the Gulf, by contrast, have much greater availability of resources on the government side. Yet even there the available resources did not always reach ordinary teachers. Prior to Qatar's radical privatisation reform of its public school system launched in 2001 (Al-Maadheed, 2017), detailed review was undertaken of existing patterns. Brewer and Goldman (2010), who were among key architects of the reform, summarised aspects of their pre-reform review. 'One surprising finding', they noted (p. 230), 'was that although Qatar is a wealthy nation, its resources were not flowing to the schools'. Teachers' salaries, they added, were relatively low, causing many to resort to private tutoring (Box 4.4). Their commentary suggested that salaries in Saudi Arabia were even lower, despite the comparable wealth in that country; and elsewhere much depended on the business models adopted by managers of private schools (see, e.g. Ridge et al., 2016).

Box 4.4   Teaching Deficiencies and Low Salaries Underpin Private Tutoring Even in a Rich Country

In 2001, Qatar embarked on radical reform of its education system. Among observations by Brewer et al. (2007, p. 29) about the need for reform was reference to a 1998 study by Al-Horr, who had surveyed influential Qataris from several segments of society:

> Respondents concurred that students were not learning the right skills in school and identified teachers as a key source of the problem. The study noted that teachers were not qualified to teach and relied on very traditional practices. According to the survey, teachers did not attempt to improve their performance at school, preferring to provide private tutoring outside the classroom.

Brewer et al. added (p. 41):

> Teacher salaries in Qatar were comparatively low. Most male teachers were expatriates, and while their average salaries were higher than those of teachers in Saudi Arabia, they were 20 percent lower than those of teachers in other GCC countries. These low wages raised questions about quality. Even if expatriate teachers were of higher quality than their salaries might indicate, they were working on a contracted basis that led to perverse incentives. Their contracts were renewed on an annual basis, fostering a continuous state of apprehension among them. And although most contracts were renewed, many expatriate teachers reported that they refrained from disciplining Qatari students for fear of offending a family with influence over hiring decisions. To supplement their low salaries, these teachers offered private tutoring outside of school, despite prohibitions against it. It has been suggested that when teachers come to rely on supplemental income from tutoring students who need extra help, they may be less inclined to provide high-quality instruction in the classroom.

Further problems related to the quality of Qatari teachers (p. 41):

> In the past, the Ministry provided incentive payments in an attempt to attract Qatari men to join the teaching profession.

> However, given the alternative – less-demanding work in higher-status government jobs – it is easy to understand why this approach failed. The Ministry then mandated that all male Qatari job applicants must spend time teaching in schools before obtaining a position in its central bureaucracy. This policy resulted in teachers who were unprepared for and dissatisfied with their teaching posts.

In some settings, private tutoring is provided through the schools. One example is from the American International School in Dubai, where the assistant principal managed a mechanism to bring the tutoring from the outside to the inside (Swan, 2010). She found that 60% of students were receiving private tutoring, especially in physics and calculus, and decided to launch a Study Support Programme through which students could receive tutoring for 50 dirhams (US$14) an hour compared with 100 to 200 dirhams outside the school. For the tutoring at 50 dirhams an hour, the school provided a matching fund of 50 dirhams an hour. The assistant principal felt that the programme enabled the tutoring to be monitored better and without fraudulent practices, and added that 'the teacher need not continue the practice in hiding for fear of being caught' (Ahmed, 2010).

Finally, at the commercial end of the spectrum, the high-income GCC countries attract more international companies, such as Kumon, Oxford Learning, Kip McGrath and Sylvan Learning, to serve relatively ordinary families.[7] They may also attract specialised operations targeting the richest of the rich. An extreme example, highlighted by the *Forbes Business* magazine (Burrows, 2015), was a tutor offering 'the Rolls-Royce of education'. This tutor even accompanied his tutees beyond the classroom, for example, on a private yacht and on travel to distant locations. Burrows observed that such tutors charge 'astronomical rates', and the rich families of the region are 'playing right into their pockets'.

Notes

1   The TIMSS question was: 'During the last 12 months, have you attended extra lessons or tutoring not provided by the school in the following subjects? a) Mathematics . . . b) Science'. Responses could include fee-free as well as fee-charging activities, though perhaps it can be assumed that most were paid for. TIMSS collects data from Grades 4 and 8, but this question was only asked to the Grade 8 students.

2   At the same time, it is worth noting Abdel-Moneim's (2021) research in Egypt. He found that large-group tutoring with 'star teachers' in affluent urban areas was equally or more expensive than small-group work with tutors who were not famous, and significantly more expensive than small-group tutoring in rural areas. This observation draws attention to social class and to geographic boundaries in discussions of the costs of private tutoring.
3   At the same time, some patterns worked in reverse: schools moved to distance learning, and some families resorted to private tutoring – face-to-face despite the dangers of infection – to cope with perceived deficiencies in school-operated distance learning (see, e.g. Abu Hammur (2020) and Mazhar (2020), writing about patterns in Jordan).
4   However, recent statistics in the GCC countries have shown higher achievement by girls than by boys. See, for example Ridge (2014) and Rocha (2018).
5   Note, however, that the definition of private tutoring included (presumably fee-free) support by parents and other family members.
6   Janaan Farhat and Munirah Eskander, Sheikh Saud bin Saqr Al Qasimi Foundation: remarks during the RCEP Policy Forum, 22 November 2021.
7   According to their websites, in 2022 Kumon had franchisees in Bahrain, Dubai and Qatar (www.kumon.org); Oxford Learning had counterparts in Kuwait and Qatar (www.oxfordlearning.com); Kip McGrath operated in Kuwait, Qatar and the UAE (www.kipmcgrath.com); and Sylvan Learning operated in the UAE, Kuwait and Saudi Arabia (www.sylvanlearning.com).

References

Abbas, Nawal (2020): 'The Private Tutoring Market Expands and the Cost of One Hour Reaches 15 Bahraini Dinar'. *Alkhalej News*, 21 December. www.akhbar-alkhaleej.com/news/article/1231209?utm_campaign=nabdapp.com&utm_medium=referral&utm_source=nabdapp.com&ocid= *Nabd_App* [in Arabic]

Abdel-Moneim, Mohamed Alaa (2021): 'In Search of a School Façade: Explaining the Centrality of Private Tutoring Among High-performing Students in Egypt'. *International Journal of Educational Development*, Vol.83, pp. 1–14.

Abdulkareem, Abbas (2015): 'A Great Demand for Private Tutoring Institutes for Many Reasons'. *Al-Dyar*, 10 July. إقبال كبير على معاهد الدروس الخصوصيّة والأسباب مُتعدّدة [in Arabic]

Abu Hammur, Muna (2020): 'Families Resort to Private Lessons to Compensate Children for the "Gap" of Distance Learning'. *Alghad*, 17 July. التعلم عن بعد "فجوة"أسر تلجأ للدروس الخصوصية لتعويض الأبناء – *Alghad* [in Arabic]

Affaneh, Izzo Ismail & El-Ajez, Fouad Ali (1999): 'The Phenomenon of the Spread of Private Tutoring in the Secondary Stage in Gaza Governorate: Its Causes and Treatment'. *Journal of Education College*, Vol.3, No.2, pp. 69–122.

Ahmed, Afshan (2010): 'Private Tutoring Becoming a Trend in the UAE'. *Khaleej Times*, 25 August. www.khaleejtimes.com/nation/general/private-tutoring-becoming-a-trend-in-the-uae

Al-Ahmad, Nizar Arafa Muhammad (1994): *The Characteristics of High School Students Who Receive Private Tutoring in Mathematics*. Masters dissertation, The University of Jordan. الخصائص المميزة لطلبة المرحلة الثانوية الذين يأخذون دروسا خصوصية في مبحث الرياضيات [in Arabic]

Al-Atrash, Khadejah Khalil (2018): 'The Role of Private Tutoring in Improving the Academic Achievement at One School in Jerusalem'. *The Guide of Scientific Research in Social Sciences* (A project to support education in Al-Quds/Jerusalem funded by Faisal Hussein Foundation), pp. 1–24. www.fhfpal.org/d-research/926.html [in Arabic]

Alawya, Sameh (2017): 'Private Tutoring Institutes are a Support to Students and a Burden on Parents'. *Lebanese Quora*, 6 April. http://lebanesequora.com/articles/333/ [in Arabic]

Albuhi, Faruq Shawqi & Alsadah, Hussain Bader (1994): 'Private Tutoring in the Educational Stages in Bahrain: Intensity, Causes and Ways to Stop it'. *Educational Journal* [Kuwait University], Vol.8, No.32, pp. 23–85. [in Arabic]

Aldaghishy, Thamir (2021): Personal Communication With Mark Bray. Saudi Arabia: Majmaah University.

Aldami, Shaza Najjeh Balash (2017): 'The Causes and Consequences of the Phenomenon of Private Tutoring: An Empirical Study in Aldewanih City [Iraq]'. *Lark Journal*, Vol.25, No.2, pp. 139–156. [in Arabic]

Alemadi, Darwish; Sellami, Abdellatif & Al-Emadi, Ahmed (2016): *Qatar Education Study 2015: Students' Motivation and Parental Participation Report*. Doha: Social & Economic Survey Research Institute (SESRI), Qatar University.

Al-Fahdeh, Muzna Bnt Khamees (2019): 'Private Tutoring: Is It a Financial and Intellectual Burden or a Means to Success?'. *Oman Daily*, 17 December. الدروس الخصوصية عبء مادي وذهني [in Arabic]

Al Farra, Samia (2009): *Private Tuition Phenomenon in Mathematics in Greater Amman – Jordan: Does Private Tuition Improve Achievement in Mathematics?*. Saarbrücken: VDM Verlag Dr. Müller.

Alhabashna, Mayser Khalil & Alnaemi, Izzeddin (2012): 'A Questionnaire Survey About the Phenomenon of Private Tutoring: The Reasons and the Educational Effects'. Jordan Country Report Presented at the Symposium on 'Private Tutoring in the Arab States: Problems and Solutions'. Cairo: League of Arab States. [in Arabic]

Al-Haj, Faten (2018): 'Private Tutoring Institutes: A Censorship-Free Business – Lebanese Are Paying for Two Schools'. *Al-Akhbar*, 1 April. https://al-akhbar.com/Education/247538 [in Arabic]

Alhawarin, Ibrahim & Karaki, Bassam Abu (2012): 'Expenditure on Private Tutoring: The Case of Jordan'. *International Proceedings of Economics Development and Research*, Vol.52, pp. 131–136.

Al-Horr, A.A. (1998): *How Elite Qataris View Educational Improvement*. Doha: Ministry of Education. [As cited by Brewer et al., 2007]

Al-Kafrawi, Mahmoud (2018): 'A Voluntary Initiative to Face the Financial Burden of Private Tutoring in Kuwait'. *Al Jazeera*, 23 December. مبادرة تطوعية لمواجهة عبء الدروس الخصوصية بالكويت [in Arabic]

Alkandari, Ahmad Jaafar (2015): 'Private Tutoring in the State of Kuwait is a Necessity but has Economic, Social and Cultural Caveats: An Analytical Study in Educational Sociology'. *Scientific Journal of the Faculty of Education* [Damietta University], No.69, pp. 68–122. [in Arabic]

Al-Khatib, Ahmed (1982): *The Phenomenon of Private Tutoring Received by Secondary School Students in Jordan*. Amman: Ministry of Education, Directorate of Planning & Educational Research. الدروس الخصوصية عند طلبة الصف الثالث الثانوي في المدارس الأردنية ظاهرة [in Arabic]

Al-Maadheed, Fatma (2017): 'Qatar: Past, Present and Prospects for Education', in Kirdar, Serra (ed.), *Education in the Arab World*. London: Bloomsbury, pp. 179–196.

Al-Marashli, Naseba (2012): 'The Reasons behind the Spread of the Phenomenon of Private Lessons According to the Headmasters, Teachers, Students and Parents and the Means by which this Phenomenon can be Stopped'. *Al-Fath Journal*, No.50, pp. 177–202. أسباب تفشي ظاهرة الدروس الخصوصية [in Arabic]

Al-Mari, Hana & Al-Khamees, Neda (2013): 'Private Tutoring: Reasons, Solutions and Its Impact on the Health of Secondary School Students in the State of Kuwait'. *Journal of Reading and Knowledge*, No.134, pp. 21–56. الدروس الخصوصية وأثرها على صحة الطلبة [in Arabic]

Alotaibi, Ghazi N. (2014): 'Causes of Private Tutoring in English: Perspectives of Saudi Secondary School Students and their Parents'. *Studies in Literature and Language*, Vol.8, No.3, pp. 79–83.

Al-Sabahi, Mounir Mohammed (2021): *The Strategic Risks of the Salary Cut Crisis in Education in Yemen: Field Research Involving 336 Educators and Academics in Eight Governorates*. Aden: Arabia Felix Center for Studies. التعليم في اليمن المخاطر الاستراتيجية لأزمة انقطاع المرتبات على

Al-Salhi, Muhsen Hamod; Malak, Badr Mohamed & Al-Kandari, Latifa Hussein (2009): 'Private Tutoring at the Secondary School Level in Kuwait: Its Nature, Causes and Solutions'. Paper for the Ninth Scientific Conference: The Challenges of Education in the Arab World (10–11 November). Faculty of Education: Minia University, pp. 1–38. https://latefah.net/artic2/dros.pdf [in Arabic]

Al-Shati, Salman & Sabti, Abbas (2012): *The Impact of Private Tutoring Costs on the Kuwaiti Family Budget*'. Elshenawy Center for Research and Studies. www.minshawi.com/?q=content/ أثر الانفاق-على-الدروس-الخصوصية-على-ميزانية-الأسرة-الكويتية [in Arabic]

Al-Yousifi, Ranim Sameer (2015): *A Suggested Vision of Managing the Crises in Secondary Schools in the Syrian Arab Republic in the Light of Some International Experiences*. PhD thesis, Damascus University. [in Arabic]

Askr, Rima & Al-Shrehi, Saja (2016): 'The Reasons for the Spread of Private Tutoring at the Secondary School Level in Deir Al-Balah'. Khawla bint Al-Azwar Secondary School for Girls, The Committee of Educational Research, Ministry of Education, pp. 1–20. انتشار ظاهرة الدروس الخصوصية للمرحلة الثانوية [in Arabic]

Bouklah, Abdullah Baker & Al-Khayal, Mouza Mohamed (1997): *A Field Study of the Phenomenon of Private Tutoring in the United Arab of Emirates*. Abu Dhabi: Department of Information and Research, Ministry of Education and Youth. الخصوصية في الامارات دراسة ميدانية لظاهرة الدروس [in Arabic]

Bray, Mark (2021d): 'Geographies of Shadow Education: Patterns and Forces in the Spatial Distributions of Private Supplementary Tutoring'. *Compare: A Journal of Comparative and International Education*, DOI: 10.1080/03057925.2021.1915749

Bray, Mark & Ventura, Alexandre (2022): 'Multiple Systems, Multiple Shadows: Diversity of Supplementary Tutoring Received by Private-School Students in Dubai'. *International Journal of Educational Development*, Vol.92, pp. 1–8.

Brewer, Dominic J.; Augustine, Catherine H.; Zellman, Gail L.; Ryan, Gery; Goldman, Charles A.; Stasz, Cathleen & Constant, Louay (2007): *Education for a New Era: Design and Implementation of K – 12 Education Reform in Qatar*. Santa Monica: RAND Corporation.

Brewer, Dominic J. & Goldman, Charles A. (2010): 'An Introduction to Qatar's Primary and Secondary Education Reform', in Abi-Mershed, Osama (ed.), *Trajectories of Education in the Arab World: Legacies and Challenges*. New York: Routledge, pp. 226–246.

Burrows, Beth (2015): 'Jetting Ahead'. *Forbes Business*, 11 October. www.forbesmiddleeast.com/en/jetting-ahead, accessed 19 January 2020.

Dabaga, Sarwat (2014): *Changing the Rules of the Game: A Case Study of Stakeholder Perceptions of the Changing Tertiary Entry Requirements in Lebanon*. EdD thesis, University of Sydney.

Enab Baladi (2019): 'Private Tutoring Flourishes in Damascus in the Lead-Up to National Exams', 6 June. https://english.enabbaladi.net/archives/2019/06/private-tutoring-flourishes-in-damascus-in-the-lead-up-to-national-exams/#ixzz6iDSSDYR8

Entrich, Steve (2021): 'Worldwide Shadow Education and Social Inequality: Explaining the Differences in the Socioeconomic Gap in Access to Shadow Education across 63 Societies'. *International Journal of Comparative Sociology*, Vol.61, No.6, pp. 441–475.

Farah, Samar (2011): *Private Tutoring Trends in the UAE. Policy Brief Number 26*, Dubai: Dubai School of Government.

Farhat, Rula (2014): 'Private Tutoring: "Dollar Is Teaching"'. *Almodoonline*, 16 October. الخصوصية: الدولار يُعلّم الدروس [in Arabic]

Ghanem, Thanaa; Zomord, Amira & Hasan, Basel (2021): 'Exploring Reasons Why Secondary Education Students Receive Private Tutoring From the Parents' Perspectives: An Empirical Study in Lattakia City'. *Tishreen University Journal for Research and Scientific Studies – Arts and Humanities Series*, Vol.43, No.5, pp. 253–274. [in Arabic]

Hatamleh, Habes M. (2021): 'The Reasons That Direct the Secondary State Students Toward Tutoring in Irbid Governorate, and Ways to Reduce Them From the Perspectives of Students and Educational Leaders and Parents'. *Educational Journal* [Kuwait University], Vol.35, Issue 138, pp. 131–171. [in Arabic] الدروس الخصوصية في محافظة إربد أسباب توجه طلبة المرحلة الثانوية العامة نحو

Hussein, Mansour G. A. (1987): 'Private Tutoring: A Hidden Educational Problem'. *Educational Studies in Mathematics*, Vol.18, No.1, pp. 91–96.

Kuwait, Ministry of Education (1962): *'Private Tutoring'. Circular No.2/100/14740* (1 December). Kuwait City: Ministry of Education. [in Arabic]

Innfrad (2016): 'The Average Spending Price of Private Tutoring in the Arab countries is 4000 Saudi Riyals in Saudi Arabia, 500 Emirati Dirhams in the UAE and 10 Kuwaiti Dinar for an Hour in Kuwait', 26 August. معدل أنفاق أسعار الدروس الخصوصية في الدول العربية [in Arabic]

Iraq, Permanent Mission to the League of Arab States (2012): A Questionnaire Survey About the Phenomenon of Private Tutoring: The Reasons and the Educational Effects'. Iraq Country Report Presented at the Symposium on 'Private Tutoring in the Arab States: Problems and Solutions'. Cairo: League of Arab States. [in Arabic]

Jamal, Ahmed Mohamed (1965): 'Perspectives and Reflections on Education and Sociology'. *Journal of Hajj and Umrah* [Saudi Arabia], Vol.8, pp. 483–484. نظرات وتأملات في محيط التربية والتعليم والاجتماع [in Arabic]

Jansen, D.; Elffers, L. & Jak, S. (2021): 'A Cross-national Exploration of Shadow Education Use by High and Low SES Families'. *International Studies in Sociology of Education*, DOI: 10.1080/09620214.2021.1880332

Jassem, Rahim & Kazem, Sami (2001): 'The Phenomenon of Private Tutoring'. *Journal of Al-Qadisiya* in Arts and *Educational Sciences*, Vol.1, No.2, pp. 39–47. ظاهرة الدروس الخصوصية [in Arabic]

Kamil, Bushra Kamal (2021): 'Attitudes of High School Students Towards Private Tutoring'. *Journal of Al-Frahedis Arts* [Tikrit University], Vol.13, No.2, pp. 397–414. اتجاهات طلبة المرحلة الثانوية نحو التدريس الخصوصي [in Arabic]

KHDA [Knowledge & Human Development Authority] (2013): *Supplementary Private Tutoring in Dubai (Unpublished Report)*. Dubai: KHDA.

KHDA [Knowledge & Human Development Authority] (2021): 'Choosing a School'. www.khda.gov.ae/en/howtochoseschool#:~:text=In%20addition%2C%20if%20 you%20are,schools%20offer%2017%20different%20curricula, accessed 19 July 2021.

Kuwait, Ministry of Education (1962): *'Private Tutoring'. Circular No.2/100/14740* (1 December). Kuwait City: Ministry of Education. [in Arabic]

League of Arab States (2012): *The Problem of Private Tutoring in the Arab Homeland*. (Background Document for the 'Seminar on Private Tutoring in the Arab World: Problems and Solutions). Cairo: League of Arab States. [in Arabic]

Mandikiana, Brian W. (2021): 'Choice and Expenditure: A Double Hurdle Model of Private Tutoring in Qatar'. *Economic Analysis and Policy*, Vol.71, pp. 1–15.

Martin, Michael O.; Mullis, Ina V.S.; Foy, Pierre & Hooper, Martin (2016): 'Performance at International Benchmarks', in *TIMSS 2015 International Results in Science*. Retrieved from Boston College, TIMSS & PIRLS International Study Center website: http://timssandpirls.bc.edu/timss2015/international-results/timss-2015/mathematics/performance-at-international-benchmarks/item-map-and-summary-of-international-benchmarks/

Mazhar, Alaa (2020): 'A Crazy Increase in the Prices of Private Tutoring and Tawjihi Students Are the Victim'. *Alghad*, 27 October. https://alghad.com/ أسعار-جنونية-للدروس-الخصوصية-وطلبة-ا [in Arabic]

New Arab (2018): 'Using WhatsApp for Tutoring in Yemen', 24 February. دروس عبر "واتساب" في اليمن [in Arabic]

Oman, Permanent Mission to the League of Arab States (2012): Oman Country Report Presented at the Symposium on 'Private Tutoring in the Arab States: Problems and Solutions'. Cairo: League of Arab States. [in Arabic]

Paracha, Zubair Naeem (2020): Saudi Edtech Noon Academy Raises $13 Million Led by STV to Accelerate Its Global Expansion'. *Menabytes*, 21 June. www.menabytes.com/noon-academy-pre-series-b/

Rahal, Maya (2017): 'A Saudi Teaching Platform Attracts a Million Students'. *Wamda*, 21 August. www.wamda.com/2017/08/saudi-teaching-platform-attracts-million-students [Arabic version: منصّة تدريس خصوصي في السعودية تنجح في استقطاب مليون طالب – ومضة (wamda.com)]

Rao, Amna Pervaiz (2017): 'Demand High for Private Tuition Despite Curbs'. *The Peninsula*, 2 April. www.thepeninsulaqatar.com/article/02/04/2017/Demand-high-for-private-tuition-despite-curbs

Ridge, Natasha (2014): *Education and the Reverse Gender Divide in the Gulf States: Embracing the Global, Ignoring the Local*. New York: Teachers College Press.

Ridge, Natasha; Kippels, Susan & Shami, Soha (2016): 'Economy, Business, and First Class: The Implications of For-Profit Education Provision in the UAE', in Verger, Antoni; Lubienski, Christopher & Steiner-Khamsi, Gita (eds.), *The Global Education Industry*. London: Routledge, pp. 264–287.

Rocha, Valeria (2018): *Beyond the Gender Gap: Improving Education for All by Minding the Differences* (Policy Brief). Sharjah: UNESCO Regional Center for Educational Planning.

Rocha, Valeria & Hamed, Sheren (2018): *Parents' Perspectives on Paid Private Tutoring in the United Arab Emirates*. Sharjah: UNESCO Regional Center for Educational Planning.

Sellami, Abdellatif (2019): *Qatar Education Study 2018: Private Tutoring Report*. Doha: Social & Economic Survey Research Institute (SESRI), Qatar University.

Sellami, Abdellatif & Le Trung, Kien (2020): 'Predictors of Parental Use of Private Tutoring in Qatar'. *International Journal of Humanities Education*, Vol.18, No.2, pp. 17–36.

Shadbash, Shahram & Albakaa, Tahir (2017): 'Iraq: An Overview', in Kirdar, Serra (ed.), *Education in the Arab World*. London: Bloomsbury, pp. 21–37.

Shamra (2020): 'The Phenomenon of Private Tutoring Is Between "a Necessity" and "Fashion" ... Some Evidence', 12 February. https://shamra.sy/news/article/d48b8f0ff1b2b919f94d1a47b5403faf. [in Arabic]

Sherman, Erline (2020): 'How Covid-19 Is a Watershed Moment for Online Tutoring'. eLearning Industry, 1 May. https://elearningindustry.com/how-covid-19-is-watershed-moment-for-online-tutoring-platforms, accessed 25 May 2021.

Suliman, Hamed & Alfakki, Mohammad (2018): 'Private Tutoring Is a Scourge ... and Its Advertisements on the Walls Is a Big Violation'. *Alarab*, 4 February. الدروس الخصوصية آفة استفحلت [in Arabic]

Swan, Melanie (2010): 'Experts Raise Doubts Over Private Tuition'. *The National*, 24 August. www.thenationalnews.com/uae/education/experts-raise-doubts-over-private-tuition-1.506737

Taeb, Azizah bint Abdullah & Falmbaan, Amal bnt Burhan (2013): 'The Phenomenon of Private Tutoring: An Empirical Study on Female Secondary School Students in Jeddah'. *Journal of Educational and Humanitarian Studies*, Vol.5, No.4, pp. 19–84. [in Arabic]

Zaman, Samihah & Al Taher, Nada (2013): 'Half of Parents Surveyed Say Children Receive Private Tutoring in Abu Dhabi'. *Gulf News*, 12 June.

Zwier, Dieuwke; Geven, Sara & van de Werfhorst (2021): 'Social Inequality in Shadow Education: The Role of High-stakes Testing'. *International Journal of Comparative Sociology*, Vol.61, No.6, pp. 412–440.

5 Educational and social impact

Learning gains

It seems obvious that the quality of the tutor is a major determinant of the extent to which a child will achieve learning gains. The challenge then for parents is to distinguish high-quality tutors from low-quality ones. Clearly the equation is not simply one of pedagogical credentials, especially since such credentials may be oriented more to schooling than to tutoring. Also important are knowledge of the subject matter, ability to link to the students' existing understanding and objectives, and interpersonal skills to establish and maintain rapport.

The corollary concerns the receptiveness and motivation of the students. Thus, no matter how well-trained and knowledgeable the tutors, few gains will be achieved if the students are excessively tired, rebellious or otherwise disengaged. Students do often respect their tutors more than their teachers, since they are paying money to the former and also have a choice. But the burden of study through both schooling and tutoring may be considerable, and may make the students tired. Also, the decision to receive tutoring may have been made by the parents rather than by the students themselves.

Further components of the equation must include the modes of tutoring. Most people assume that one-to-one tutoring is the best model; but students can benefit from peers in small groups or even in large classes. Indeed, the fact that some 'star tutors' command classes exceeding 100 students usually reflects the skills and certainly the charisma of such tutors, which, in turn, enhances student motivation. Thus, evaluation should not instantly dismiss large-class tutoring in favour of small groups or one-to-one tutoring. Internet tutoring may also have good effectiveness if well delivered and received.

Taking these matters further, various statistical surveys have endeavoured to assess learning gains from tutoring while controlling for other

DOI: 10.4324/9781003317593-5

variables. Yet as noted by Guill et al. (2020, p. 283) after reviewing the literature, 'empirical findings on the effectiveness of private tutoring are rather contradictory'. Some researchers (e.g. Berberoğlu & Tansel, 2014) have found a positive impact in some subjects, but others have found minimal effects or none at all (e.g. Park et al., 2016; Ryu & Kang, 2013). Bearing in mind the importance of including qualitative factors in the analysis, Guill et al. (2020) investigated German data to see if relationships could be found between the quality of tutoring and the motivation of students. They did not find clear correlations with academic achievement, but did identify reductions in stress felt by tutored students.

Concerning research in the countries addressed by the present study, one of the few pertinent items is by Al Farra (2009) and addresses mathematics in Jordan. Al Farra conducted a pair of studies, first focusing on a sample of students in government schools who provided information on mathematics achievement before and after receiving tutoring, and second focusing on a parallel sample of students in an elite school offering International Baccalaureate curricula. She did find an increase in scores among the government students receiving tutoring, but remarked (p. 88) that conclusions could not be generalised because of incomplete information on the students not receiving private tutoring and the possibility of other factors, such as enhanced maturity, contributing to scores. The second study found no improvement after private tutoring.

In such circumstances, rarely can families always be certain of the direct value of their investments. Much depends on contexts and on the actors in the ecosystem. Indeed decision-making can be a challenge even for parents with detailed knowledge. Thus, Al Farra (2009, p. 316) interviewed a researcher who had himself conducted detailed investigation of private tutoring in Jordan (Al-Batsh, 1999). Asked whether he felt that private tutoring could improve academic achievement, the interviewee replied with personal experience:

> My daughter (Class 12) took more than 60 hours of tuition in Mathematics in a centre last year and her grade after private tuition did not change. I know of more students who did not benefit from many hours of private tuition as well.

Others might similarly be sceptical of tutors, particularly when they claim to be multifunctional for all needs (Figure 5.1) and lack training for their roles. Indeed critics may highlight the dangers not only of time being wasted with inadequate tutors but also of students learning bad habits, including dependence on tutoring and neglect of school lessons (Suliman & Alfakki, 2018).

Figure 5.1 The Tutor Who Can Do Everything?
Source: Abdullah Jaber, Riyadh. Reproduced with permission.

Nevertheless, Al Farra kept the door open on this matter (2009, p. 140), still highlighting the potential value of mentoring and the possibility that private tutoring could improve achievements 'under certain conditions pertaining to the tutee, tutor, duration and environment'. Moreover, regardless of whether private actually improves academic achievement, surveys commonly indicate that it is perceived to do so. Thus, among the 49% of surveyed students across 14 schools in Dubai who received tutoring (KHDA, 2013), 86% 'agreed' or 'strongly agreed' that tutoring improved their examination grades; and when a sample of UAE parents were asked by Rocha and Hamed (2018) about improvement of their children's performance after receiving tutoring, they responded as shown in Figure 5.2. Among students with 'excellent' pre-tutoring performance, 67% were said to have improved 'a lot'. Among students with 'good' performance, that proportion was only 39%; and the proportions fell further to 28% and 30% among students with 'medium' and 'poor' performance. Nevertheless, students in all categories were perceived to have improved 'somewhat' or 'a lot'.

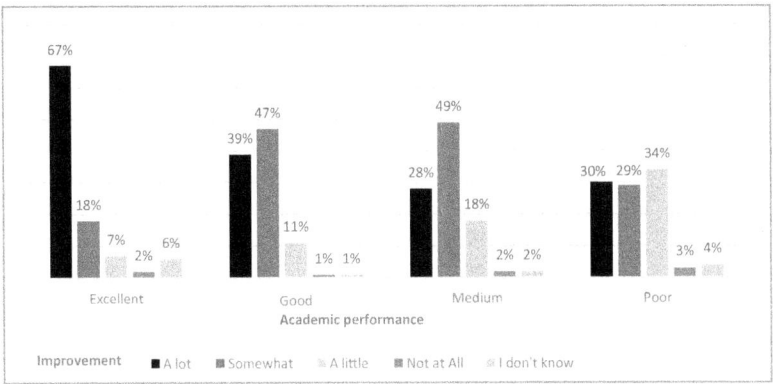

Figure 5.2 Parental Perceptions of Change in Overall Academic Performance After Private Tutoring, UAE.

Source: Rocha and Hamed (2018), p. 26.

Backwash on schooling

A further complexity is that private tutoring is not simply a neutral shadow; rather, it has a backwash on the system that it imitates. Private tutoring may subtract as well as supplement.

One way in which tutoring has a backwash concerns the performance and attitudes of classroom teachers. When many students receive supplementary support, teachers may assume that those needing such support are indeed receiving it, and may then put less effort into their teaching than otherwise they would. Such actions then become self-fulfilling – students realise that indeed they have to seek supplementary support if they are to keep up with peers.

Related to this matter, classroom dynamics may be shaped by hidden elements of favouritism. This was mentioned in Syria, for example, by Youssef (2021). Teachers may praise students who know the answers and who keep up with or exceed the learning of their peers, while unconsciously (or even consciously if the teachers have vested interests) neglecting or sending negative vibrations to those who lag behind.

On the other hand, students who receive tutoring may be bored in class or even defiant – perhaps encouraged in such defiance by the tutors. As explained by a teacher in Qatar to Suliman and Alfakki (2018), tutors may incite students not to listen to their class teachers in order to encourage dependence on the tutors. 'In such cases', the teacher added, 'the students tend not to maintain calm in the classroom, which will have negative effects on the achievement of their fellow students'. Students may even decide to skip schooling, instead relying on their tutors. As noted by Alayan (2014) in Jordan, these students 'feel like they don't need to bother going to class, since their tutor will tell them what they really need to know'.

Teachers who are also tutors may additionally find their days tiring, and devote less attention to their mainstream lessons than otherwise they would; and even more disturbing are occasions in which teachers deliberately cut the content of their mainstream lessons in order to push their existing students to receive supplementary tutoring from them outside school hours. Sometimes the teachers even leak to their tutees the questions that those teachers will set in school-based tests. As explained by one parent in Saudi Arabia (Al-Mukhtar, 2010): when her son went to ask his teacher to explain something, the teacher offered private lessons.

> The teacher came almost every day and charged us around SR4,000 (US$1,060) a semester. What surprised us is that at the end of the semester he told us that if we paid him SR2,000 more, then he would give my son the questions for the final exam and help him with the answers.

A similar remark was made by a parent in Dubai who was also a teacher and whose daughter was in Grade 10 (Shahbandari, 2012):

> As an educationist, I understand that tutoring students privately is very important for those students who are considered weak in studies, and who are not able to get help from their parents but when school teachers leak out exam papers to students at tuition classes it affects those students who are working hard on their own.

Such practices have been widely criticised as a form of corruption (Abu Aneez, 2010; Affaneh & El-Ajez, 1999; Al-Fahdeh, 2019; Al-Loah, 2015; Shelbaya, 2018); and the irony in this case was that the parent was feeling pressurised by the system of private tutoring even though as a teacher she was able to help her own daughter.

Social values

The aforementioned examples about corruption show that private tutoring may shape the values not only of the participants but also of the non-participants. More positively, when it works well, private tutoring can enhance not only learning itself but also the excitement of learning. Further, it can help to keep young people constructively occupied rather than at a loose end and in danger of pursuing anti-social activities. This indeed is among the non-educational objectives of some parents.

However, private tutoring is more likely to have problematic sides, among which many have been stressed in the literature. One is that students may become dependent on tutoring, which they see in utilitarian terms as a way to avoid labour that should be part of the educational process for their own depth of learning. As remarked by one parent in Bahrain (quoted by Abbas, Ja'afar, 2020), if parents provide excessive support through tutors, 'the child will gradually view tutors as "domestic helpers" or private drivers and servants whose tasks are to make the child feel fully relaxed from examinations and homework'. A similar comment was presented in Oman by Al-Fahdeh (2019): 'Tutoring can make a student not interested in exploring further about specific information'.

Perhaps among the most obvious implications is that official statements about fee-free education for equality of education are hollow when in effect payment for supplementary education becomes obligatory. Students also see the commercialised values of some teachers and of many tutors. A few tutors endeavour to work themselves out of a job in the sense of providing support to students so that after a while those students can look after themselves, but many other tutors deliberately encourage dependence in order to maintain their revenues. Further, as remarked by Alkandari (2015, p. 70) with specific reference to Kuwait but with broader relevance: 'The whole process confirms the tendency to purchase educational certificates for children [rather than] learning and education'.

Also underlying this phenomenon is a damaging dimension of meritocracy. Sandel (2020, p. 95) has stated that in the USA and Europe, 'disdain for the poorly educated is more pronounced, or at least more readily acknowledged, than prejudice against other disfavored groups'. Social dynamics are, of course, different in the Middle East, but it remains the case that many people who gain social status from high academic achievement feel that they deserve that status from having earned it rather than recognising that they had advantages of adequate family finance to pay for private tutoring.

Finally, private tutoring on a one-to-one basis, especially when in the homes of the tutors, may bring risks of sexual misdemeanours. In Dubai, Mustafa (2011) reported on 'a series of court cases involving tutors accused of molesting their pupils'. In one specific case, a male non-national clerk was accused of molesting three girls that he had been tutoring for several years. Similarly, in Bahrain Taref (2017) reported on a male non-national teacher who was sentenced to a year in prison followed by deportation after molesting a female student during private tutoring; and comparable issues have been raised in Palestine by Muslim (2009). The gender segregation in dominant Middle East cultures may limit this problem compared with other parts of the world, but the issue still deserves note.

References

Abbas, Ja'afar (2020): 'Private Tutoring Is a Necessity Rather Than "Prestige" '. *Akhbar Al Khaleej*, Vol.26. الدروس الخصوصية ضرورة وليست وجاهة [in Arabic]

Abu Aneez, Yusra (2010): 'Private Tutoring Is a Lifeline for the Student in the Sea of High School'. *Jordanzad*, 1 April. الدروس الخصوصية طوق نجاة للطالب في بحر الثانوية العامة [in Arabic]

Affaneh, Izzo Ismail & El-Ajez, Fouad Ali (1999): 'The Phenomenon of the Spread of Private Tutoring in the Secondary Stage in Gaza Governorate: Its Causes and Treatment'. *Journal of Education College*, Vol.3, No.2, pp. 69–122.

Alayan, Aya (2014): Why Aren't Jordanian Children in School? *Al-FanarMedia*, 3 December. www.al-fanarmedia.org/2014/12/arent-jordanian-children-school/ [Arabic version: الصفوف المدرسية خالية من الطلاب في الأردن]

Al-Batsh, Muhammad Walid (1999): 'Evaluating Individuals' Perceptions About Private Tutoring in the Jordanian Society'. *Dirasat: Educational Sciences*, Vol.36, No.2, pp. 342–368. [in Arabic]

Al-Fahdeh, Muzna Bnt Khamees (2019): 'Private Tutoring: Is It a Financial and Intellectual Burden or a Means to Success?'. *Oman Daily*, 17 December. الدروس الخصوصية عبء مادي وذهني [in Arabic]

Al Farra, Samia (2009): *Private Tuition Phenomenon in Mathematics in Greater Amman – Jordan: Does Private Tuition Improve Achievement in Mathematics?*. Saarbrücken: VDM Verlag Dr. Müller.

Alkandari, Ahmad Jaafar (2015): 'Private Tutoring in the State of Kuwait Is a Necessity but Has Economic, Social and Cultural Caveats: An Analytical Study in Educational Sociology'. *Scientific Journal of the Faculty of Education* [Damietta University], No.69, pp. 68–122. [in Arabic]

Al-Loah, Amr (2015): 'Private Tutoring in Gaza: A Phenomenon That Kills Creativity and Equals Between "Who's Good and Who's Bad" '. *SHMS News Agency*, 7 January. الدروس الخصوصية بغزة [in Arabic]

Al-Mukhtar, Rima (2010): 'Private Tutors Make Money as Final Exams Draw Near'. *Arab News*, 10 June.

Berberoğlu, Giray & Tansel, Aysit (2014). 'Does Private Tutoring Increase Students' Academic Performance? Evidence from Turkey'. *International Review of Education*, Vol.60, pp. 683–70

Guill, Karin; Lüdtke, Oliver & Köller, Olaf (2020): 'Assessing the Instructional Quality of Private Tutoring and Its Effects on Student Outcomes: Analyses From the German National Educational Panel Study'. *British Journal of Educational Psychology*, Vol.90, pp. 282–300.

KHDA [Knowledge & Human Development Authority] (2013): *Supplementary Private Tutoring in Dubai* (Unpublished report). Dubai: KHDA.

Muslim, Abdalhadi (2009): 'Private Tutoring in Gaza Has Advocates and Opponents'. *Donia Alwatan*, 19 April. الدروس الخصوصية بغزة ما بين المؤيد والمعارض [in Arabic]

Mustafa, Awad (2011): 'Private Tutors Are Illegal, Parents Told'. *The National*, 16 January. www.thenationalnews.com/uae/education/private-tutors-are-illegal-parents-told-1.354696

Park, Hyunjoon; Buchmann, Claudia; Choi, Jaesung & Merry, Joseph J. (2016): 'Learning beyond the School Walls: Trends and Implications'. *Annual Review of Sociology*, Vol.42, pp. 231–252.

Rocha, Valeria & Hamed, Sheren (2018): *Parents' Perspectives on Paid Private Tutoring in the United Arab Emirates*. Sharjah: UNESCO Regional Center for Educational Planning.

Ryu, Deockhyun & Kang, Changhui (2013): Do Private Tutoring Expenditures Raise Academic Performance? Evidence from Middle School Students in South Korea'. *Asian Economic Journal*, Vol.27, No.1, pp. 59–83.

Sandel, Michael J. (2020): *The Tyranny of Merit: What's Become of the Common Good?*. New York: Allen Lane.

Shahbandari, Shafaat (2012): 'School over? Time for Tutorials'. *Gulf News*, 23 June. https://gulfnews.com/uae/education/school-over-time-for-tutorials-1.1039199

Shelbaya, Farah (2018): 'Private Tutoring Is a Trade That Exceeded the Limits of 1,000 Dinars Each Semester'. *Alanbat News*. سقف تجاوزت تجارة الخصوصية الدروس الـ1000 دينار للفصل الواحد [in Arabic]

Suliman, Hamed & Alfakki, Mohammad (2018): 'Private Tutoring Is a Scourge . . . and Its Advertisements on the Walls Is a Big Violation'. *Alarab*, 4 February. الدروس الخصوصية آفة استفحلت [in Arabic]

Taref, Ali (2017): 'Court: One year in Prison and Deportation From Bahrain of an Egyptian Teacher Who Harassed a Female Student'. *Alwasat News*, 12 May. الحبس سنة والإبعاد عن البحرين لمعلم مصري تحرش بطالبة [in Arabic]

Youssef, Samar (2021): 'The Phenomenon of Private Tutoring in the Basic Education Stage in Light of Some Variables: A Field Study for a Sample of the First Cycle Students in Jablah District'. *Tishreen University Journal for Research and Scientific Studies – Arts and Humanities Series*, Vol.43, No.3, pp. 263–282. [in Arabic]

6 Policy implications

Designing and enforcing regulations

Regulations for tutoring may be divided into two main groups, which are here considered in turn. First are regulations on whether, and under what circumstances, serving teachers may provide private tutoring; and second are regulations on tutorial centres. Some of the countries considered here have more detailed regulations than others. Among considerations when drafting regulations is capacity for enforcement. Such capacity needs both adequate political acceptability and personnel with ability to identify and follow-up contraventions. The extent of capacity arguably needs consideration at the design stage, since situations in which regulations are disregarded may be worse than situations of no (or minimal) regulations.

Regulations concerning provision of private tutoring by serving teachers

Table 6.1 presents information from 10 of the 12 countries considered in this study. No information could be secured by the authors on regulations in Lebanon and Yemen, and their administrations seemed to be in the laissez-faire category.[1]

A useful place to commence analysis is with the models that permit teachers to provide remunerated tutoring under certain circumstances, namely those in Saudi Arabia, Qatar, Jordan and the UAE. Each model has distinctive features.

- *Saudi Arabia*. The structures through which teachers are permitted to provide private tutoring are called Educational Services Centres, and may be established on a semester-by-semester basis and during schools' long vacations. Teachers can provide the tutoring through the

DOI: 10.4324/9781003317593-6

Table 6.1 Regulations on Teachers Concerning Private Supplementary Tutoring in Middle East Countries

Bahrain	A 2011 Ministerial Resolution (No.517/MAN/2011AD) provided for evening remedial lessons in schools, determining fees and group sizes. Teachers were not permitted to tutor in the evening the students that they had taught during the day. Beyond this in-school provision, tutoring by serving teachers was officially banned (Najeeb, 2016).
Iraq	A 2012 Ministry of Education circular (No. 8800) prohibited serving teachers from providing private tutoring. Punishment for infringement, in line with 1991 rules on state employment, included demotion. A 2017 follow-up Ministry of Education circular (No. 963) instructed school administrations to secure written statements from teachers at the beginning of each academic year that they would not provide private tutoring. The instruction was repeated in a 2018 circular (No. 8112). A 2020 circular (No. 5285) added that teachers who had resigned from distinguished schools in order to provide tutoring were forbidden to use the names of those schools for marketing purposes.
Jordan	The Secretary General of the Ministry of Education has reportedly stated that any teacher giving private tutoring without official approval violates Civil Service regulations (Obeidat, 2017). However, teachers can provide tutoring in officially approved strengthening centres.
Kuwait	According to Al-Sowelan (2013, p. 14), as early as 1961 a circular to schools from the Majlis Al-Maaref (Council of Knowledge), which preceded formation of the Ministry of Education in 1962, prohibited individual tutoring 'because of its harmful effect on students'. It was followed by a Ministry of Education circular (Kuwait, 1962), and a further directive (Kuwait, 1964) that teachers were prohibited from providing private tutoring unless they had explicit permission from the Ministry. A 1982 circular reported on establishment of two Ministry-funded but fee-charging centres (one for boys and one for girls) providing remedial support for upper secondary students in an effort to remove the need for private tutoring (Kuwait, 1982). However, these measures were not effective, and in 1999, a committee was formed to consider the issues (Kuwait, 1999; Al-Mari & Al-Khamees, 2013). In 2014, a new circular banned all private tutoring on the grounds that it was a financial burden on families and discouraged effort by students during school lessons (Trenwith, 2014). Concerning implementation, in 2016 for example 13 teachers were arrested for providing tutoring in a café (Toumi, 2016). Another circular in 2017 stressed the illegality of private tutoring by expatriate teachers (Kuwaiti Education Agent, 2017). Nevertheless, in 2018, the Ministry of Education responded differently to a proposal in the National Assembly to eliminate private tutoring through a law. The Ministry stated its belief 'that the phenomenon of private tutoring does not require a law that increases punishment for those who are responsible', and instead advocated further improvement of schooling to make tutoring unnecessary (Kuwait, Ministry of Education, 2018). Recommended measures included further curriculum reform, issuing of licences to teachers in public and private sectors, and deployment of media to spread appropriate messages to parents and others.

(*Continued*)

64 Policy implications

Table 6.1 (Continued)

Oman	The Civil Service Act (Oman, 2007) requires government personnel to 'keep the dignity of the job' (Article 102.B) and not 'exploit [the] job to gain personal benefits' (Article 103.I). In line with this, regulations have been issued for example in Dhofar Governorate in 2017 (Al-Rawahi, 2017; Al-Sinania, 2018). The circular indicated intent to follow strict legal procedures in the event of teachers providing private tutoring, and urged headteachers to give the matter serious attention. Subsequent press coverage (e.g. *Arab News*, 2018) highlighted a 'private tuition ban' particularly as it applied to Indian teachers.
Palestine	Ministerial decree No. 5 (2010) banned private tutoring. It made a link to Articles 83/84 of the Civil Service Act, which stated that government personnel may not have additional jobs without the permission of their Division heads.
Qatar	According to the vice-president of the Qatari Bar Association (quoted by Mukhtar, 2015), Article 19 in Chapter 4 of the 1994 penal code prohibited teachers from providing out-of-school tutoring. The penalty for doing so would be imprisonment for up to six months and a fine of not less than 10,000 riyals (US$2,700). Law No. 18 of 2010 confirmed criminalisation of unlicensed tutors (Raslan, 2020). However, teachers were permitted to provide school-supervised tutoring under certain conditions (Abdurrahman, 2018). Newly recruited teachers are commonly informed in writing about the legal framework when they sign their contracts (Sellami, 2021).
Saudi Arabia	Teachers in both public and private schools are permitted to provide private tutoring if done through school-supervised educational centres (Aldaghishy, 2021; Saudi Arabia, 2015). Private tutoring by teachers outside this channel is prohibited.
Syria	Legislative Decree No. 73 (2011) stated that Ministry of Education employees, including teachers and principals, were banned from work in private tutoring institutes (Al-Boselh, 2018; Al-Omar, 2019). Ministry of Education Circular No.7686 issued in 2018 forbade mainstream teachers from working in tutorial institutes and from preparing curriculum material for such work (Syria, 2018; Muraselon, 2019). Actions in 2021 included prosecution of teachers for providing private tutoring, even in their homes (Al-Nasser, 2021; Musa, 2021).
United Arab Emirates	Farah (2011, p. 5) stated that while the Ministry of Education forbade teachers from tutoring their own students, no formal law existed. More recently, a 2019 initiative reported by Rizvi and Al Amir (2019) envisaged allowing teachers in government schools to offer private tutoring 'in a new drive to improve standards'. Teachers could register to provide one-to-one lessons for pupils from schools other than their own, and would be paid by the Ministry. It was designed to apply only to public schools.

centres either in their schools or in the students' homes. Conditions set out in regular circulars (e.g. Saudi Arabia, 2015) include that:

- the instruction may be for remediation or enrichment;
- tutoring may be one-to-one or in groups, with a maximum group size of 15 students;
- tutoring sessions should last one hour for students in intermediate and secondary grades, and 45 minutes for students in primary grades;
- teachers may use science and computer laboratories for teaching;
- standard fees should be charged according to the mode and level of education;[2]
- revenues should be divided between the teachers and other persons involved;[3] and
- allowance should be made for the social and financial circumstances of individual students, if necessary reducing or exempting fees in liaison with the school guidance and counselling committees.

This system has existed for several decades, and private tutoring outside this framework is officially prohibited. However, the prohibition is widely ignored, especially by non-national teachers for whom the traditions of tutoring both in their home countries and in Saudi Arabia are long-standing and for whom there is strong incentive because their salaries are generally lower than those of nationals.

- *Qatar*. The model for enrichment learning classes in some respects resembles that in Saudi Arabia. As described by Abdurrahman (2018), teachers are permitted to provide instruction outside working hours under the direct supervision of their school administrations. The Ministry of Education and Higher Education permits two types of such classes – general and special. General classes should serve 8 to 15 students, while special classes should have only 1 to 4 students. School administrations are expected to supervise the operations and to select appropriate teachers. Students, who may be from across the range of abilities, are permitted to choose their teachers within the pool.
- *Jordan*. As long ago as 1977, the Ministry of Education established a system for supplementary classes in government schools during the long summer vacation (Jordan, 1977a), and accompanying regulations allowed for remuneration of teachers on a fixed scale (Jordan, 1977b). In due course this innovation was displaced, in part by cultural centres that were permitted to offer private tutoring in academic subjects. In 2008, the Ministry of Education was reportedly in dispute

with parliamentarians over the possibility of these centres providing tutoring (*Khaberni News*, 2008). A crack-down in 2014 (Jordan, 2014) asserted that cultural centres should focus on non-academic activities such as sewing and computer use, and dozens of centres were closed for 'violating the Ministry's regulations and laws' in the domain of academic tutoring (Obeidat, 2017). To replace the tutoring function, the Ministry cooperated with sub-national Directorates of Education to open 'strengthening centres' in which secondary students could secure instruction from distinguished teachers who were paid 10 dinars (US$14) per hour by the Ministry of Education. Nevertheless, some cultural centres continued with academic tutoring (Mazhar, 2020; Shelbaya, 2018).

- *UAE*. In 2012, a model for after-school study centres was launched in Sharjah as 'an effort to curb illegal private tutors' (Ahmed, 2012). Many teachers were providing tutoring in the marketplace but faced the risk of being dismissed or even going to court if apprehended. As such, in Ahmed's (2012) view, the new centres represented 'a less risky way to boost their income'. The architects of the scheme asserted that the centres would have higher quality than much tutoring: 'Many times the teacher may not provide the right information and that will affect the child's performance. These centres will be monitored so they will have to offer quality teaching'. Prices were kept at just 250 dirhams (US$68) per month, compared with 200 dirhams per hour commonly charged by tutors.

The models represented by these cases are not easy to operate. Teachers in the government-run centres are commonly remunerated at lower rates than they could receive externally, and the managers do not have incentives comparable to the profit-earning motives of entrepreneurs in the private sector. For such reasons, one model in Palestine that had been launched in 2010 was abandoned. As remarked to Al-Loah (2015) by one government interviewee, 'this programme had not received students' support or encouragement and hence we closed these centres'.

The Jordanian government-sponsored educational centres were launched as a complement to the policy of prohibiting serving teachers from providing tutoring. Table 6.1 shows that comparable prohibitions have been launched in Iraq, Kuwait, Oman, Qatar, Saudi Arabia, Syria and the UAE. Figure 6.1 illustrates the administrative mechanisms with an Iraqi circular. However, private tutoring has in practice continued in all these countries. Policy makers have in some countries made periodic pushes to sound warnings and revitalise attention to the issues, but their admonitions have usually had only short-term impact. Authorities have had to grapple with

Figure 6.1 Iraq Ministry of Education Circular on Private Tutoring, 2017.

strong currents and tacit objections not only by teachers but also by students and their parents. In that connection, Syrian dissent with the 2017 ban of private tutoring deserves note (Zamanalwsl, 2017). Three hundred students staged a sit-in outside the United Nations building to protest. Some students' families then joined, turning the event into 'a demonstration that roamed the streets'. Subsequent media reporting was very critical of judicial police searching teachers' houses to eradicate private tutoring. It led to a partial policy shift in which the Minister of Education stated that under Syrian Legislative Decree No. 7 of 2017 such searches should be confined to unlicensed tutorial institutes, and that the penalty of 500,000 lira, which was the equivalent of a teacher's salary for a whole year, was only applicable to unlicensed institutes (*Jesr Press*, 2020).

Regulations on tutorial centres

Concerning tutorial centres, in all countries, standard business regulations may be assumed to apply concerning accounting, contracts, taxation and so on, alongside building regulations about fire escapes, electrical wiring and toilets. In addition, some countries – but relatively few – have specific regulations for tutorial centres (Table 6.2).

Table 6.2 Regulations on Private Tutorial Centres in Middle East Countries

Iraq	The minimum staffing of tutorial centres, as set by Ministry of Education regulations, is three people with bachelor's degrees, among whom at least one graduate must be from an education programme (Iraq, 2021). Premises must have at least two rooms with at least 1.5 square metres per student. Separate entrances by gender should be available if the institute serves both genders.
Lebanon	A licencing system for tutorial centres does exist (Al-Haj, 2018), but it is widely ignored (see below).
Qatar	Detailed regulations have been promulgated on the establishment and operation of centres, including prices (Qatar, 2015, 2017) (see below).
Syria	Legislative Decree No. 35 of 2010 (Syria, 2010; see also Alsheikh Ali, 2019), building on Decree No. 55 of 2004 (Syria, 2004; see also Al-Boselh, 2018), required properties for private tutoring to be licensed. The stipulated penalty for infringement was 50,000 lira, or double that sum in the case of repetition. In 2017, the Democratic Union Party administration announced a decision to ban all private tutoring including that in tutorial centres (Zamanalwsl, 2017).

Among these regulations, those in Qatar are the most detailed. They state (Qatar, 2015, 2017):

- Applicants for licences must be at least 21 years of age, with no criminal record, not employed by the Ministry of Education and Higher Education, and provide a bank guarantee of 100,000 riyals (US$27,500).
- Licences are valid only for designated premises, and can only relate to alternative premises with written approval. The areas must be commensurate with the number of learners according to norms by the competent department.
- No persons can be appointed to work in a centre without written approval from the competent authority. The director must have a high qualification appropriate for the centre activities, and experience of at least five years. Tutors must have a higher qualification in the field of specialisation and experience in that specialisation of at least three years.
- Managers must maintain data on courses and other services.
- Prices must be displayed in a visible location at the headquarters.

A fine of up to 100,000 riyals could also be imposed for incorrect information on the façade of a centre's headquarters or publications. Penalties for other offences allowed for imprisonment for up to six months or a fine of up to 100,000 riyals. Licences needed renewal on an annual basis.

Having set out these regulations, the Qatar authorities moved even further. In 2019, they devised a system to evaluate and classify all accredited centres, and announced that the licence of any centre gaining a poor evaluation would be suspended (Al-Sharq, 2019). The authorities also set price ceilings for tutoring at 250 riyals per month and 150 riyals at the primary level, and announced that they would perform surprise inspections. Then in 2020, three further conditions were set for licencing of a tutorial centre (Raslan, 2020), namely:

- the building must have at least six classrooms;
- the centre must cater for all educational stages (primary, intermediate and secondary), and both male and female students; and
- each tutorial group should comprise no less than ten students.

These requirements considerably reduced the number of institutions. In 2020 the country had only 94 licensed tutorial centres (Raslan, 2020), compared with 608 schools (Qatar, 2020).

Also worth mentioning is specific action in the UAE at the time of the Covid-19 outbreak. Having closed the schools, the Ministry of Education also took the logical step of closing face-to-face tutoring in tutorial centres and by individual tutors (Al-Amir, 2020). The action illustrates the pertinence of emergency regulations in certain circumstances.

In contrast to these measures is the largely laissez-faire situation in Lebanon. Although a licencing system does exist, spokespersons from the Ministry of Education acknowledged to Al-Haj (2018) that most tutorial centres operated without licences and that 'we do not know what exactly we should do'. The spokespersons stressed that such centres were 'not authorised and not subject to any censorship' because the Ministry had no information on enrolments or earnings – or, it seemed, on curriculum or other matters. As noted by another interviewee, while teachers were accountable to their schools and the Ministry, 'the private tutor is not questioned'.

Worth adding is that none of the countries covered by this study had any regulations on tutoring provided by university students, retirees or other informal suppliers. The absence of regulations for this category matches the global picture, since such suppliers are indeed difficult to monitor and control. An alternative approach for authorities in some countries around the world, which of course could also apply to tutorial centres and to teachers who provide tutoring, is to encourage consumer awareness among parents (Bray & Kwo, 2014, pp. 53–55).

Making private tutoring less necessary

Alongside regulations should be efforts to make private tutoring less necessary. It will never disappear, because families are competitive and tutoring helps them to get ahead and stay ahead. For this reason, as mentioned earlier, private tutoring has even emerged in the Nordic countries that are renowned for the quality and orientations of their education systems (Christensen & Zhang, 2021). Nevertheless policy makers, especially in the well-resourced systems, can pay attention to teachers' salaries to remove any argument that they are underpaid, can review class sizes, and can improve staff quality and performance within schools. They can also bring issues into the open to discuss not only with teachers but also with parents and other stakeholders in order to reach consensus on the best way forward for society as a whole.

Beyond these broad dimensions are issues related to the structure and functioning of education systems. Concerning high-stakes examinations, for example, care is needed to avoid simplistic recommendations about alternative modes of assessment since examinations are commonly considered equalising in the sense that the goal posts are the same for all candidates (Au, 2009; Kellaghan & Greaney, 2019). Potential reform of high-stakes examinations also needs to recognise that their major purpose is to sort students into different tracks and perhaps push some students out of the education system altogether. In this connection, experiences in the Republic of Korea are worth noting. The authorities there, faced by the negative impact of high-stakes examinations, sought to replace the examinations by lotteries first at the transition to lower secondary schooling and then at the transition to upper secondary schooling (Kim, 2016, p. 21). The experiment was abandoned in the face of public dissent, especially from families who felt that their children were denied the reward for their hard work in academic achievement. It also created challenges for schools that had to manage greater diversity in the standards of their intakes. For the present study, moreover, many students – especially in the GCC countries – are non-nationals taking examinations from their home countries; and even the nationals may take examinations, such as the International Baccalaureate (IB) and the International General Certificate of Secondary Education (IGCSE), set by external bodies.

Nevertheless, policy makers should at least be sensitive to the impact of high-level examinations set by both their own administrations and others, and within national education systems can seek ways to balance final evaluations through school-based assessments of project work and other performance measures. Further, while high-stakes examinations seem essential at the end of secondary schooling, they may be less necessary at earlier stages. In this connection, Kellaghan and Greaney (2019, pp. 28–29) noted that Jordan, Kuwait and Yemen were among MENA countries that had abolished exit examinations at the level of basic education.[4]

Broader curriculum matters are also pertinent, including the orientation and density of content. In Palestine, Affaneh and El-Ajez (1999) stated that the curriculum was heavily influenced by Egyptian models that were less relevant to Palestinian students; and throughout the region, teachers commonly blame the density of official curricula for inability to achieve full coverage during regular lessons (Aldami, 2017; Al-Haj, 2018; Al-Omar, 2018; Raoof & Hamo, 2017). Alayan (2014), quoting a student in Jordan, stated: 'Teachers explain very quickly because they want to finish the curriculum. But, most of the time, we can't understand in the classroom and need to have some private lessons'. In Kuwait, Al-Mekrabi et al. (2011, p. 4) stressed the need to pilot proposed new textbooks, to determine their positive and negative dimensions and implications for tutoring.

At the same time, teachers' delivery styles may be called into question. Thus, Alayan's (2014) view on the Jordanian situation seemed to resonate with that of another interviewee: 'We should not forget to talk about the traditional teaching style'. Particularly, this interviewee felt, new technology could provide tremendous information and engagement for students, but 'Jordanian teachers are still generally stuck using blackboards and chalk at schools'. During the period since this observation was made, technology advanced even further with great speed. However, it is doubtful whether standard teaching styles moved with comparable speed. Indeed, the tutoring industry is likely to have been more nimble than schooling, bringing corresponding increase in attractiveness of tutoring to students.

In their defence, teachers commonly and legitimately point to class sizes, especially in the lower-income countries. In Syria, for example, teachers have highlighted the challenges of managing classes of over 50 students (Shamra, 2020); and the same point has been made in Bahrain even with classes of 30–35 students (Innfrad, 2016). In Iraq, a strategy to reduce class size has been operation of double and even triple shifts for over one third of students (UNICEF, 2017a, p. 13);[5] and proportions of multiple-shift schools are even higher in Palestine (UNICEF, 2017b).[6] However, the shift system compromises learning, especially for the students in afternoon sessions when both teachers and students are less alert. Moreover, even with the double and triple shifts, many schools in Iraq and Palestine still had classes of 50 or more students.

Yet while large classes are clearly an obstacle to individual attention of the sort that can be secured in private tutoring, patterns elsewhere show that reduction in class size might not be a simple solution. Thus, Saudi Arabia in the mid-2010s had an average teacher to pupil ratio of just 1:9 (Aldaghishy, 2019, p. 40), yet still had very high rates of private tutoring (Al-Zeyoudi, 2016; Taeb & Falmbaan, 2013). Much tutoring in that country was driven by long-standing traditions, originally reflecting cultures brought by teachers from Egypt, Palestine, Syria and elsewhere. It also reflected normalisation of the practice as experienced by families.

Turning to other dimensions, a further government way to reduce private tutoring could be through provision of public tutoring. Most obviously this can be done by schools themselves, that is, by providing extra support without charge, but it can also be provided externally. Internationally, the Khan Academy (*www.khanacademy.org*) has become well-known as a resource bank, and some governments have developed counterpart websites to fit national curricula. In Oman, for example, in order to achieve what one author called 'eliminating the greed of private tutoring' (Abu Kalila, 2021, p. 2), the government launched a website (*www.omtut.com*) with video recordings available at a nominal cost. Separate sections are devoted to biology, chemistry, English, mathematics, physics and social studies. A related initiative presents live broadcasts in which teachers explain their subjects in detail, and students anywhere can follow and then communicate with the teachers by audio and video. These sessions are recorded, so can be revisited; and the system provides continuous electronic examinations for students to assess their own performance. Similar projects have been launched in Kuwait (Kuwait, 1999; Al-Mutairi, 2016), Qatar (Abdurrahman, 2018) and Syria (Al-Boselh, 2018). They have not replaced private tutoring, but at least they have provided some alternatives.

Engaging in partnerships

Long experience not only in the Middle East but also around the world shows that in this domain, as in most others, Ministries of Education cannot do everything by themselves. Partnerships are necessary both within and beyond the government machinery.

Beginning with partnerships between *branches of government*, a few examples illustrate possibilities and productive avenues.

- The *Ministry of Labour* becomes involved when non-national personnel require work permits for tutoring. Particularly in the GCC countries, attention has focused on non-nationals providing tutoring without work permits and thus in contravention of the labour laws (see, e.g. Nasr, 2013; Mahmoud & Al-Dhafiri, 2021).
- The *Ministry of Economy* or equivalent may collaborate on regulations for tutorial centres, focusing on the business dimensions of their work, including contractual arrangements, taxation and advertising. The authorities in Qatar have sought to prohibit advertising of private tutoring by non-licensed entities (Al-Mohammadi, 2017), and the vice-president of Qatari Bar Association (quoted by Mukhtar, 2015) has stated that 'any advertisement in newspapers or elsewhere must be authorized by the Ministry of Economy'. If this applies to each and

every advertisement, it does not seem workable; but calling attention to the matter could at least make both the tutors and the organisations distributing the advertisements more cautious.
- The administrations of sub-national *Governorates* and *Emirates* can also usefully co-ordinate with each other. For example, in 2017 Dhofar Governorate in Oman followed the lead of Muscat Governorate in a circular prohibiting teachers from providing tutoring (Al-Rawahi, 2017), showing some solidarity and coordination across the country. In the UAE, KHDA regulations on schools in Dubai instilled general confidence and encouraged parents in neighbouring Sharjah to enrol in Dubai schools. However, the KHDA also regulated tutorial centres more strictly than counterparts in Sharjah. The result was a morning flow of Sharjah students to Dubai for schooling, and an afternoon flow of Dubai students to Sharjah for private tutoring.[7]

Secondly, governments can and should liaise with *teachers' unions*. While these bodies generally exist to safeguard teachers' interests, especially concerning salaries and conditions of service, the bodies are also concerned with the reputation and prospects for the profession as a whole. Experience elsewhere shows that while teachers' unions do wish to protect the opportunities of their members (i.e. teachers in regular schools) to earn extra incomes, they also wish to protect schools from competition with tutorial centres. This perspective has been evident, for example, in Cambodia, India and Malaysia (Bray & Kwo, 2014, pp. 58–59). It is also evident in statements by the global body, Education International, which counts nearly 400 teachers' unions among its members (see, e.g. Silova, 2012; Stromquist, 2018).

Liaison with teachers' unions can also bring pertinent messages to the government side. When the Syrian government in 2010 announced its prohibition of private tutoring by serving teachers, the measure was relatively acceptable because average teachers' monthly salaries were around 20,000 lira (US$450). However, teachers' remuneration was then sharply eroded by inflation and inadequate compensatory increases. Thus, in 2019 salaries appeared to have risen to reach an average of 25,000 lira, but they were then worth only the equivalent of US$50 (Syrian Days Net, 2019). This matter again returns to salaries and the costs of living. In Kuwait, according to Al-Kafrawi (2018), the monthly salary of most teachers in private schools was between 160 and 300 dinars (US$526–980) yet rents for two-room apartments were commonly 220 and 400 dinars. The cost of private tutoring was said to start from 10 dinars per session to primary school students and reach 30 dinars in higher grades. Some families paid tutors specific amounts for the whole academic term, for example, reaching 500 dinars in physics for secondary school students. Policy makers clearly need to take account of such arithmetic in their calculations.

A third important partnership is with *parents*. The fact that private tutoring is ongoing reflects demand from parents as much as supply from teachers, entrepreneurs and self-employed tutors. As such, dialogue will be most effective when policy makers recognise that fact rather than just making declarations about manipulation, corruption and so forth. All parents want the best for their children, yet a useful distinction can be between parents who seek tutoring because their children really need it to keep up with their peers, and parents who want tutoring for enrichment and keeping ahead in the race. Government personnel can help parents to secure clarity in their goals and strategies, and to decide what is really in the best interests of their children. Ministries of Education can operate advisory websites and channels for information and complaint. These processes may empower the parents as consumers and in the process shape the actions of the suppliers of tutoring. Box 6.1 reports the perhaps surprising fact that 45% of sampled parents in the UAE did not know the qualifications of the tutors that they had hired. This seems to suggest that parents could be encouraged to become more critical and discerning consumers.

The fourth category of partnership concerns *schools*. Some schools are directly administered by governments, while others are private institutions that nevertheless operate under government oversight. Dialogue with school administrations can elucidate perspectives and proposals for action, and schools can themselves bring teachers and parents into the picture. Review of patterns within and across Middle East countries shows wide divergence of school-level perspectives on private tutoring. Some schools prefer to ignore the phenomenon, viewing it as beyond their control and responsibility, while other schools try to control it through institutional policies, and a few schools actively encourage private tutoring as a way to earn revenue

---

Box 6.1   How Clearly Do Parents Know What They Are Getting?

The research in UAE by Rocha and Hamed (2018) included questions to 1,487 parents. When parents were asked about aspects that they considered important when hiring tutors, top of the list, at 86%, were 'skills and experience' (p. 28). However, when asked about the educational level of the last tutor they had hired (p. 26), 45% did not know.

and reward their teachers. Again, governments would be wise to recognise this diversity when engaging in dialogue. The observation also shows that school-level policy makers are important alongside their counterparts at higher levels. School-level policies on private tutoring may be especially effective because teachers, parents and students are known people rather than just anonymous statistics.

The next category for partnership concerns the *media*. In former times this implied printed newspapers, radio or television, but in contemporary times it mainly means electronic communications. Journalists on the one hand seek to attract attention through dramatic stories, but on the other hand seek everyday narratives that resonate with readers' lives. The number of references to media reports in the present study reflects the value of this channel. Governments can and should put forth their own perspectives through official websites and speeches, and they can also encourage dialogue through the media that may reach further than their own channels.

Partnerships may also be developed with *organisations and individuals committed to social development*. For example, in Yemen a body called Hadarmawt Foundation for Human Development was established in 2006 to provide remedial support for secondary school students (Al-Saqqaf, 2010). It provided resources to remunerate teachers, while only charging students if they showed inadequate commitment. To manage the students' side, an initial fee was charged and then reimbursed on successful completion of the programme. A different type of arrangement concerns individual teachers who are willing to provide free tutoring. Al-Kafrawi (2018) cited one example in Kuwait. A parent, Al-Kafrawi reported, approached a history teacher to request support for her daughter prior to the final secondary school examination. The teacher did not wish to charge money, and tweeted general willingness to offer free tutoring. The matter attracted public attention, with colleagues expressing willingness to help and other respondents offering classrooms. These initiatives were independent of government roles, but could still be publicised by the authorities.

Governments may even collaborate with *entrepreneurs in the tutorial sector*, urging them to engage in self-regulation. Professional associations of private tutoring in Asia and elsewhere include self-regulation in their roles both to enhance trust in the industry and to reduce the threat of external regulation (Bray & Kwo, 2014, p. 56–57). The Australian Tutoring Association (ATA), for example, has a code of conduct to which members are expected to adhere (Australian Tutoring Association, 2015).[8] Bodies of this type have not yet been established in the countries covered by the present report, and in Dubai, for example, efforts during the 2010s to encourage self-regulation were disappointing.[9] Nevertheless, the idea should be kept on the table as

76 Policy implications

a possibility. Self-regulation could focus on such matters as advertising, contracts, ethics and perhaps even pricing.

Finally, governments may collaborate with *researchers* in universities and elsewhere. While the present study has been able to draw a general picture, many details are lacking. Both quantitative and qualitative research is valuable to show the scale, nature and implications of private tutoring, together with trends over time. University-based researchers are always keen to have audiences for their work and to demonstrate impact. In addition to review of existing studies, governments can commission new studies.

Notes

1. Concerning Yemen, this remark was confirmed by the Ministry of Education who responded to the (2021) RCEP questionnaire on the subject.
2. In 2015, the standard fees were: (a) for groups, 100 riyals (US$27) per month per subject for elementary students, 150 riyals for intermediate students, and 200 riyals for secondary students; (b) for one-to-one tutoring in the centre, 50 riyals per session for elementary students, 60 riyals for intermediate students, and 70 riyals for secondary students; (c) for one-to-one tutoring in the students' homes, 80 riyals per session for elementary students and 100 riyals for intermediate and secondary students.
3. A table of percentages showed the revenue distribution between the school principal, counsellor, teacher, servant and the Ministry of Education Department of Guidance and Counselling. The largest proportions were allocated to teachers: 65% for groups, 75% for one-to-one tutoring in the centres, and 85% for one-to-one tutoring in the students' homes. Respective proportions for principals were 13%, 7.5% and 5%. For counsellors, they were 10%, 7.5% and 5%; and for the Department of Guidance and Counselling, they were 7%, 10% and 5%. The servants received 5% of group-tutoring revenue, but were not remunerated for the other categories.
4. Other MENA countries that had abolished exit examinations at this level included Djibouti, Morocco and Tunisia. By contrast, as reported by Kellaghan and Greaney (2019, p. 29), Algeria, Egypt, Saudi Arabia and Syria had retained them.
5. In 2015/16, proportions of schools with double or triple shifts in the Iraq Centre were 35.3% at the primary level, 30.7% at lower secondary, and 30.6% at upper secondary. In the Kurdistan region, they were 32.4% in basic education and 35.7% in upper secondary (UNICEF, 2017a, p. 13).
6. According to UNICEF (2017b), in the Gaza Strip 70% of UNRWA schools and 63% of public schools had double shifts. In addition, six schools (but with indication in the report of the percentage that they represented) had triple shifts.
7. Mark Bray, field observations, 2012.
8. The ATA website presents the Code of Conduct in 13 languages, to cater for different language groups in the country. It adds in red font: 'In the event of an ATA member not following the code of conduct then an investigation may follow, which could lead to suspension and/or expulsion'. https://ata.edu.au/about-us/member-code-of-conduct/, accessed 29 June 2021.
9. Information from KHDA at various junctures, 2012–2018.

References

Abdurrahman, Amr (2018): 'Five Alternatives to Limit Private Tutoring'. *Al-Sharq*, 9 May. بدائل للحد من الدروس الخصوصية [in Arabic]

Abu Kalila, Hadiya Muhammad Rashad (2021): 'Alternatives to Limit Private Tutoring in Light of the Experiences of Some Countries'. *Journal of the Faculty of Education* [Damietta University], Vol.36, No.77, pp. 1–14. بدائل للحد من الدروس الخصوصية علي ضوء تجارب بعض الدول [in Arabic]

Affaneh, Izzo Ismail & El-Ajez, Fouad Ali (1999): 'The Phenomenon of the Spread of Private Tutoring in the Secondary Stage in Gaza Governorate: Its Causes and Treatment'. *Journal of Education College*, Vol.3, No.2, pp. 69–122.

Ahmed, Afshan (2012): 'Centres Will Stamp Out Illegal Teachers'. *The National*, 12 January. www.thenationalnews.com/uae/education/centres-will-stamp-out-illegal-teachers-1.399734

Al-Amir, Noura (2020): 'Private Tutoring Faces Fines and Demands to Double Them on Parents'. *Albayan Across the UAE*, 31 October. الغرامات تواجه الدروس الخصوصية ومطالب بمضاعفتها بحق أولياء الأمور [in Arabic]

Alayan, Aya (2014): Why Aren't Jordanian Children in School? *Al-FanarMedia*, 3 December. www.al-fanarmedia.org/2014/12/arent-jordanian-children-school/ [Arabic version: الصفوف المدرسية خالية من الطلاب في الأردن]

Al-Boselh [Newspaper] (2018): 'The Ministry Has Adopted Procedures to Control the Phenomenon of Private Tutoring'. [Syria], 29 November. [Arabic version: الوزارة تتخذ اجراءات للحد من الدروس الخصوصية]

Aldaghishy, Thamir (2019): *The Influence of the Global Education Reform Movement on Saudi Arabia's Education Policy Reforms: A Qualitative Study*. PhD dissertation, St Louis University.

Aldaghishy, Thamir (2021): Personal communication with Mark Bray. Saudi Arabia: Majmaah University.

Aldami, Shaza Najjeh Balash (2017): 'The Causes and Consequences of the Phenomenon of Private Tutoring: An Empirical Study in Aldewanih City [Iraq]'. *Lark Journal*, Vol.25, No.2, pp. 139–156. [in Arabic]

Al-Haj, Faten (2018): 'Private Tutoring Institutes: A Censorship-Free Business – Lebanese Are Paying for Two Schools'. *Al-Akhbar*, 1 April. https://al-akhbar.com/Education/247538 [in Arabic]

Al-Kafrawi, Mahmoud (2018): 'A Voluntary Initiative to Face the Financial Burden of Private Tutoring in Kuwait'. *Al Jazeera*, 23 December. مبادرة تطوعية لمواجهة عبء الدروس الخصوصية بالكويت [in Arabic]

Al-Mari, Hana & Al-Khamees, Neda (2013): 'Private Tutoring: Reasons, Solutions and Its Impact on the Health of Secondary School Students in the State of Kuwait'. *Journal of Reading and Knowledge*, No.134, pp. 21–56. الدروس الخصوصية وأثرها على صحة الطلبة [in Arabic]

Al-Mekrabi, Mohammed Abdul Rahim; Afifi, Mohammed Abbas; Abdullah, Hessein; Warak, Safaa & Alenzi, Aisha (2011): *The Phenomenon of Private Tutoring [in Kuwait]: Causes and Solutions (Unpublished Report)*, Kuwait City: Ministry of Education [in Arabic].

Al-Mohammadi, Hassan (2017): 'Ministry of Education: Advertisements for Unlicensed Private Tutoring Are Banned'. *Al-Shorouk Newspaper*, 16 February. وزارة التعليم: إعلانات الدروس الخصوصية ممنوعة بدون ترخيص. [in Arabic].

Al-Mutairi, Abdulrahman Eid (2016): 'Evaluate the Effectiveness of Kuwaiti Educational Channel Programs in the Light of Their Objectives'. *Journal of Wadi Al-Neel for Research and Studies*, Issue 9, pp. 89–134. تقويم فاعلية برامج قناة التربوية الكويتية [in Arabic]

Al-Nasser, Mahdi. (2021). 'The minister of education in Syria asks the police to prosecute private tutors'. 2 March., *7a.net*, وزير التربية يطلب الشرطة لملاحقة أساتذة الدروس الخصوصية. [in Arabic].

Al-Omar, Mary (2019): A Winning Market Whose Customers Are Students at Key Transition Points in Their Education: The Revival of Private Tutoring in Damascus Before Exams. *Enab Baladi*, 26 May. الدروس الخصوصية تنتعش في دمشق [in Arabic]

Al-Rawahi, Issa (2017): 'Private Tutoring Has Crossed a Red Line'. *Al-Roya*, 22 November. الدروس الخصوصية تتجاوز الخطوط الحمراء | جريدة الرؤية العمانية (alroya.om) [in Arabic]

Al-Saqqaf, Ahmad Muhammad Abdallah (2010): 'Evaluation of the Remedial Classes Programme for High School Students in Hadarmawt Governorate in the Republic of Yemen'. *Journal of the Gulf and Arabian Peninsula Studies*, Issue 138, pp. 50–107. تقويم برنامج حصص التقوية لطلبة نهاية المرحلة الثانوية في محافظة حضرموت اليمنية [in Arabic]

Al-Sharq (2019):'5000 Riyals Fine for Education Centres that Don't Achieve the Requirements', 4 December. غرامة للمراكز التعليمية المخالفة للاشتراطات [in Arabic].

Alsheikh Ali, Hind (2021): 'The Ministry of Education: The Majority Know the Laws That Ban Private Tutoring in Houses and the Judicial Police will be Strict'. *SHAM FM*, 26 July. شام اف ام (sham.fm) [in Arabic]

Al-Sinania, Suad (2018): 'Private Lessons: Psychological Phenomenon or Educational Necessity?'. *Oman Daily*, 26 December. الدروس الخصوصية.. ظاهرة نفسية أم ضرورة تعليمية؟ – الموقع الرسمي لجريدة عُمان (omandaily.om) [in Arabic]

Al-Sowelan, Zoha'a F. (2013): 'Factors Related to the Spread of Private Tutoring in the Secondary School Unified System in Kuwait'. *The Education Journal*, Vol.27, Issue 107, pp. 13–52. عوامل انتشار ظاهرة الدروس الخصوصية بدولة الكويت [in Arabic]

Al-Zeyoudi, Majed Mohamed (2016): 'Saudi Families' Perceptions Towards Private Tutoring in the Light of Some Demographic Variables'. *Journal of Arab Gulf Mission*, No.141, pp. 69–87. الدروس االخصوصية لدى الأسر السعودية [in Arabic]

Arab News (2018): 'Oman Calls Out Expat Teachers Who Breach Private Tuition Ban', 3 September. arabnews.com

Au, Wayne (2009): *Unequal by Design: High-stakes Testing and the Standardization of Inequality*. New York: Routledge.

Australian Tutoring Association (2015): *Code of Conduct*. Sydney: Australian Tutoring Association. https://ata.edu.au/wp-content/uploads/2019/11/ATA-Code-of-Conduct.pdf

Bray, Mark & Kwo, Ora (2014): *Regulating Private Tutoring for Public Good: Policy Options for Supplementary Education in Asia*. Hong Kong: Comparative Education Research Centre, The University of Hong Kong, and Bangkok: UNESCO. https://cerc.edu.hku.hk/books/regulating-private-tutoring-for-public-good-policy-options-for-supplementary-education-asia/

Christensen, Søren & Zhang, Wei (eds.) (2021): *Shadow Education in the Nordic Countries*. Special issue of *ECNU Review of Education* [East China Normal University], Vol.4, No.3. www.roe.ecnu.edu.cn/f9/1d/c12911a391453/page.htm

Farah, Samar (2011): *Private Tutoring Trends in the UAE* (Policy Brief Number 26). Dubai: Dubai School of Government.

Innfrad (2016): 'The Average Spending Price of Private Tutoring in the Arab Countries is 4000 Saudi Riyals in Saudi Arabia, 500 Emirati Dirhams in the UAE and 10 Kuwaiti Dinar for an hour in Kuwait', *26 August*. معدل أنفاق أسعار الدروس الخصوصية في الدول العربية [in Arabic]

Iraq, Ministry of Education (2017): *'Private Tutoring'. Circular No.963* (23 January). Baghdad: Ministry of Education. [in Arabic]

Iraq, Ministry of Education (2021): 'Summary of Conditions for Opening a Private Institute'. Baghdad: Ministry of Education. [in Arabic]

Jesr Press (2020): 'An Inspection Operation was Carried out in "the Bedrooms" in Tartous, Searching for Private Tutoring', 25 March. تفتيش غرف نوم مدرسين في طرطوس بحثاً عن الدروس الخصوصية [in Arabic]

Jordan, Ministry of Education (1977a): *The System of Summer Studies in Public Schools, Issued in Accordance with Article 117 of the Education Law No.16 of 1964 (Regulation No.30)*. Amman: Ministry of Education.

Jordan, Ministry of Education (1977b): *Organizing Summer Studies in Public Schools Issued in Accordance with Article 6 of Regulation No.30 of 1977' (Instruction No.15)*. Amman: Ministry of Education.

Kellaghan, Thomas & Greaney, Vincent (2019): *Public Examinations Examined*. Washington: The World Bank.

Khaberni News (2008): 'The Ministry of Education and Parliamentarians Face Off over Private Tutoring', 11 March. التربية والنواب يتواجهان على الدروس الخصوصية [in Arabic]

Kim, Young-Chun (2016): *Shadow Education and the Curriculum and Culture of Schooling in South Korea*. New York: Palgrave Macmillan.

Kuwaiti Education Agent (2017): 'Legal Procedures Will Be Taken Regarding Private Tutoring'. *Kuwait News Agency*, 22 January. www.kuna.net.kw/ArticleDetails.aspx?id=2588269&Language=ar [in Arabic]

Kuwait, Ministry of Education (1962): *'Private Tutoring'. Circular No.2/100/14740* (1 December). Kuwait City: Ministry of Education. [in Arabic]

Kuwait, Ministry of Education (1964): *'Private Tutoring'. Circular No.1/100/7884* (14 October). Kuwait City: Ministry of Education. [in Arabic]

Kuwait, Ministry of Education (1982): *Implementation of the Recommendations of the Committee to Study and Treat the Phenomenon of Private Tutoring* (21 January). Kuwait City: Ministry of Education. [in Arabic]

Kuwait, Ministry of Education (1999): *'Formation of a Higher Committee to Produce Remedial Lessons for Science and Maths on Television for the Secondary Stage'. Decree No.23459* (11 October). Kuwait City: Ministry of Education. [in Arabic]

Kuwait, Ministry of Education (2018): 'A Proposal From a Law From the Honorable Member of the National Assembly, Walid Al-Tabtani, Regarding the Regulation of Private Tutoring'. *Reference 620988*, 16 September. [in Arabic]

Mahmoud, Ashraf Arabi Khalil & Al-Dhafiri, Iman Muhammed Jadee (2021): *Report About the Phenomenon of Private Tutoring and Ways to Limit Its Spread in the State of Kuwait*. Kuwait: Educational Research and Curriculum Sector, Ministry of Education.

Mazhar, Alaa (2020): 'A Crazy Increase in the Prices of Private Tutoring and Tawjihi Students Are the Victim'. *Alghad*, 27 October. https://alghad.com/أسعار-جنونية-للدروس-الخصوصية-وطلبة-ا/ [in Arabic]

Mukhtar, Mahmoud (2015): 'The Punishment of Private Tutoring Dealers Is to Be Prison'. *Alarab*, 6 October. السجن ينتظر تجار الدروس الخصوصية [in Arabic]

Muraselon (2019): 'The Ministry of Education Issued a Strict Statement on Private Tutoring in Syria', 3 January. وزير التربية يصدر تعميم شديد اللهجة بخصوص التدريس في سوريا [in Arabic]

Musa, Zaid (2021): 'The Ministry of Education in the Syrian government prosecutes teachers because of private tutoring'. *North Press Agency*, 3 March. وزارة التربية في الحكومة السورية تلاحق المعلمين بسبب الدروس الخصوصية [in Arabic]

Najeeb, Sarah (2016): 'Private Tutoring Is Banned and the Violators Are Referred to Investigation'. *Alayam News*, 27 May. الدروس الخصوصية ممنوعة وتحويل المخالفين للتحقيق [in Arabic]

Nasr, Yasmeen (2013): 'Private Tutors Threatened With Deportation From Saudi Arabia'. *Savidati*, 12 January. معلمو الدروس الخصوصية مهددون بالترحيل من السعودية [in Arabic]

Obeidat, Malik (2017): 'Education: Emphasis on Preventing Private Tutoring – and Closing Any Cultural Centers that are Violating it'. *Jo24*, 21 March. تشديد على منع الدروس الخصوصية [in Arabic]

Oman, Sultanate of (2007): *Civil Service Law Issued by Royal Decree (120/2004) as amended until November 2007*. Royal Decree 120/2004. Muscat: Ministry of Civil Service. https://omanportal.gov.om/wps/wcm/connect/29e415b6-d845-452d-8d8b-537f53a57b81/Civil+Service+Law.pdf?MOD=AJPERES&CACHEID=29e415b6-d845-452d-8d8b-537f53a57b81

Qatar, Government of (2015): *Law No.18 on Organising the Practice of Educational Services, 2015*. Doha: Government of Qatar. www.almeezan.qa/LawArticles.aspx?LawTreeSectionID=17000&lawId=6749&language=ar [in Arabic]

Qatar, Ministry of Education and Higher Education (2017): *The Decision of the Minister of Education and Higher Education No.10 of 2017 Regarding the Practice of Educational Services*. Doha: Ministry of Education and Higher Education. [in Arabic]

Qatar, Ministry of Education and Higher Education (2020): *Annual Statistics of Education in the State of Qatar 2017–2018*. Doha: Ministry of Education and Higher Education.

Raoof, Tamara & Hamo, Khlood Yousef (2017): 'The Spread of Tutoring in Iraq's Institutions: Causes and Factors'. *Journal of Kirkuk University for Administrative and Economic Sciences*, Vol.7, No.1, pp. 252–270. انتشار ظاهرة التعليم الخصوصي في مؤسسات العراق: الأسباب والعوامل [in Arabic]

Raslan, Mahrous (2020): 'During a Meeting With Officials of the Ministry of Education: Service Centres call for Combating Private Tutoring'. *Al-Raya*, 8 August. مراكز الخدمات تطالب بالتصدي للدروس الخصوصية. [in Arabic]

Rizvi, Anam & Al Amir, Salam (2019): 'UAE to Legalise Private Tutoring to Improve Standards in Schools: The New Scheme Applies Only to Teachers at Public Schools'. *The National*, 25 April. www.thenationalnews.com/uae/education/uae-to-legalise-private-tutoring-to-improve-standards-in-schools-1.853516

Rocha, Valeria & Hamed, Sheren (2018): *Parents' Perspectives on Paid Private Tutoring in the United Arab Emirates*. Sharjah: UNESCO Regional Center for Educational Planning.

Saudi Arabia, Ministry of Education (2015): *Circular to All Male Students' Schools (In Relation to Establishing Centres for Educational Services in the Second Semester of the Academic Year 1436–1437 Hijri)*. No. 37183709, 22/01/1437 Hijri. Riyadh: Ministry of Education. [in Arabic] [Parallel Circulars Sent on a Regular Basis for Each Semester, and Also to Female Students' Schools]

Sellami, Abdellatif (2021): Personal Communication with the Authors. *College of Education, Qatar University*, 10 December.

Shamra (2020): 'The Phenomenon of Private Tutoring is between "A Necessity" and "Fashion" ... Some Evidence', 12 February. https://shamra.sy/news/article/d48b8f0ff1b2b919f94d1a47b5403faf. [in Arabic]

Shelbaya, Farah (2018): 'Private Tutoring is a Trade that Exceeded the Limits of 1,000 Dinars each Semester'. *Alanbat News*. الدروس الخصوصية تجارة تجاوزت سقف الـ1000 دينار للفصل الواحد [in Arabic]

Silova, Iveta (2012): *Hidden Privatisation(s) in Public Education: The Case of Private Tutoring*. Brussels: Education International. www.ei-ie.org/en/item/21194:hidden-privatisations-in-public-education-the-case-of-private-tutoring

Stromquist, Nelly P. (2018): *The Global Status of Teachers and the Teaching Profession*. Brussels: Education International. http://ei-ie-al.org/sites/default/files/docs/2018_ei_research_statusofteachers_eng_final.pdf

Syria, Government of (2004): *Legislative Decree No.55* [Regulating private educational institutions for pre-university education]. Damascus: Government of Syria. www.parliament.gov.sy/arabic/index.php?node=5567&cat=16525 [in Arabic]

Syria, Government of (2010): *Legislative Decree No.35* [Banning use of unlicensed premises for private tutoring]. Damascus: Government of Syria. المرسوم التشريعي 35 لعام 2010 الذي يحظر استخدام العقارات والأماكن غير المرخصة *(parliament.gov.sy)* [in Arabic]

Syria, Ministry of Education (2018): *Circular No.7686/435* [On curriculum, Intellectual Property and Private Tutoring]. Damascus: Ministry of Education. [in Arabic]

Syrian Days Net (2019): 'Private Tutoring in Syria is Prohibited without Licence', 16 February. في سورية الدرس الخصوصي ممنوع إلّا برخصة/ [in Arabic]

Taeb, Azizah bint Abdullah & Falmbaan, Amal bnt Burhan (2013): 'The Phenomenon of Private Tutoring: An Empirical Study on Female Secondary School Students in Jeddah'. *Journal of Educational and Humanitarian Studies*, Vol.5, No.4, pp. 19–84. [in Arabic]

Trenwith, Courtney (2014): 'Kuwait bans private tutors'. *Arabian Business*, 14 October. www.arabianbusiness.com/kuwait-bans-private-tutors-567811.html

UNICEF (2017a): *The Cost and Benefits of Education in Iraq: An Analysis of the Education Sector and Strategies to Maximise the Benefits of Education*. New York: UNICEF.

UNICEF (2017b): 'Right of Education for 1 Million Palestinian Children at Risk'. Press Release, 11 September. www.unicef.org/sop/press-releases/right-education-1-million-palestinian-children-risk

Zamanalwsl Net. (2017): 'The People of Qamishli Protest Against the Decision of Democratic Union Party (PYD) to Ban Private Tutoring', 7 August. أهالي القامشلي يحتجون على قرار منع الدروس الخصوصية. [in Arabic]

7 Conclusion

Understanding the big picture

Commonalities and diversities

This study commenced by noting the long-standing global existence of shadow education and its recent dramatic expansion. In societies as diverse as India, Greece, Japan, Mauritius and Russia, the literature has noted the existence of private supplementary tutoring even during the late 19th century and early 20th centuries. Yet only in the last quarter of the 20th century, and accelerating during the 21st century, has private tutoring attracted strong attention. This remark applies to the Middle East as much as to other world regions.

The book has also stressed the significance of contextual commonalities and differences for comparative analysis. Perhaps the most significant commonality, Chapter 3 suggested, is the globalised model for schooling with primary and secondary sections, grades, term-times/vacations, classrooms, trained teachers and examinations at watershed points. Such features, the chapter added, are so standardised that they are often taken for granted. They help to explain why most patterns in the Middle East have counterparts around the world. Schools in all contexts bring together stakeholders with converging but also competing interests. These stakeholders have always included governments, teachers, families and students, and now include increasing numbers of entrepreneurs. The existence of these stakeholders in all systems underpins the commonalities, and variations in the roles and powers of the stakeholders help to explain the differences.

Beyond the global picture is a regional one. The 12 countries on which this study focuses form a group that differs from other groups and has its own commonalities and differences. The commonalities include the role of Arabic and cultural traits associated with religion. The most obvious differences lie in economics, with the six GCC countries having high incomes

DOI: 10.4324/9781003317593-7

especially from oil, and the other six countries having much lower per capita incomes. Political and economic differences are also evident between and within these two sub-groups (Abdel-Moneim, 2016, p. 53). Education systems have themselves sometimes been the arena for political challenge and social upheaval. In some respects private tutoring has acted as a safety valve through which families manage shortcomings in education systems through their own actions, but in other respects it has been a flashpoint and a focus for resentment and protest.

Further variations are evident within individual countries. Matching patterns across the world, variations in the scale and nature of shadow education are striking between rural and urban locations and between localities inhabited by different socio-economic classes. More distinctive to the GCC countries are variations in shadow education arising from the consumption patterns of nationals and non-nationals. Most strikingly, nationals in both Qatar and the UAE comprise only 13% of the total populations, and the proportion in Dubai within the UAE is only 9%. These numbers reflect the ability of governments, businesses and households to employ many non-nationals for economic development and other purposes, which in turn has had far-reaching implications for both schooling and shadow education (Bray & Ventura, 2022). Separate school systems serve multiple nationalities in the GCC countries, commonly with striking differences in both the scale and nature of private tutoring. The other countries also have much diversity, for example with Lebanon's system of consociation permitting variations in schooling for different religious and other groups. More investigation is desirable to find the implications for shadow education in this situation. Similar remarks might be made about the impact in Syria and Iraq of the regimes that dominate different parts of those countries. Yet the fact that the broad contours of shadow education are similar within and across both GCC and other countries again underlines the commonalities in the goals, structures and management of education systems across the range of economic and political circumstances.

Related to the aforementioned picture, the analysis shows the significance of historical forces and imported traditions. Within the broader MENA region, Egypt has by far the largest population and exerts a very strong influence throughout the Arabic-speaking world. The GCC countries in particular have employed many Egyptian teachers, who have brought with them their cultures including those relating to private tutoring. The Egyptian influence has also been felt strongly in Jordan, Palestine, Syria and other countries of the region. Yet imported traditions have also been of many other types, visible in the wide array of private schools serving non-national populations. Thus, elaborating on the UAE example, the schools serving Indian communities are heavily influenced by traditions in India, while similar remarks may apply to schools following curricula from France, Germany, Iran, Japan, Pakistan, the Philippines, the UK and other countries. This observation underlines the pertinence of the shadow metaphor – that in many ways private tutoring not only mimics the official curricula but is also shaped by the broader cultures of the communities that it serves.

Turning back to commonalities, gender issues as they relate to Islamic culture also deserve remark. In contrast to earlier periods of history, the balances of genders receiving private tutoring seem largely equal or even in some locations favouring females. Less information is available on the gender of tutors and on the ways in which the different genders perform their work. Informal evidence suggests that Syria has more female than male tutors, chiefly because many males have left the country to avoid being conscripted to the army in the context of civil war. Such factors may also be evident in other locations experiencing armed conflict, but again the GCC and other relatively stable countries such as Jordan would have different dynamics.

Among the GCC countries, instructive data on gender are available from Qatar. In 2017/18, 70.1% of teachers in public schools were female, and only 29.0% were male (Qatar, 2020, p. 50). Even more strikingly, among the Qatari teachers females comprised 93.1% while males comprised just 6.9%. El-Emadi et al. (2019, p. 11) quoted a (male) principal to help explain this pattern:

> Most males here in Qatar do not like teaching jobs . . . this is why we don't have many male teachers, they prefer to work in high managerial professions, in business or as military officers. Therefore, they don't have passion for teaching; most females, however, have passion for teaching which is associated with cultural and social issues that characterize a conservative society.

This has implications for both schooling and tutoring. Another (male) principal quoted by El-Emadi et al. (2019, p. 11) pointed out: 'Cultural issues are very sensitive, not only students feel uncomfortable being taught by an opposite gender, teachers as well feel the same'. And, a further (male) interviewee remarked:

> You rarely find a female teacher worried about financial issues; on the contrary most male teachers are concerned and look for extra earning through private tutoring; therefore, they put more efforts on private tutoring

This last remark would seem to refer mainly to non-Qatari male teachers; yet these non-Qatari male teachers comprised only 27.3% of the total teaching force in public schools. The national survey reported by Sellami (2019, p. 12) indicated that 45% of public school students in Grades 8, 9, 11 and 12 were receiving private tutoring. The report did not provide a breakdown of Qatari and non-Qatari enrolments by gender and by public/private schooling, but the overall picture showed male enrolment rates of 42% and female ones of 38%. This seems to imply that large proportions of female students in public schools were receiving tutoring, and raises the question about who was providing this tutoring and how.

Thus, further research would be desirable in Qatar and elsewhere not only on the genders of students but also on the genders of tutors. It could include investigation of tutoring styles to complement data already showing differences in classroom teaching styles across genders (El-Emadi et al., 2019). It could also include data on prices charged. In Hungary, Bíró (2020) found that female tutors charged less than males, raising the question why that was the case and whether it was a self-imposed gender bias. A similar question could usefully be asked in Qatar, elsewhere in the Middle East, and beyond.

Roles of the state and of the market

As remarked in Chapter 3, in all countries considered here, in common with the global picture, governments and the public accept and expect that the state should hold the main responsibility for schooling at least of national students. Increasing numbers of national families do opt for private schooling, usually because they desire improved quality and specific curricula. Non-national families may not be eligible for public schools but do also have choices in the types of private schools attended. Nevertheless, public education systems under the supervision of national Ministries of Education are the core.

At the same time, Middle East countries have to some extent followed other parts of the world in efforts to strengthen market forces within public systems. This was especially evident in 2001 when Qatar launched a reform that transformed its public schools into Independent Schools comparable to the Charter Schools in the USA (Brewer & Goldman, 2010), though the reform was partially reversed in 2016 (Abdel-Moneim, 2020). In Saudi Arabia, a counterpart reform was launched in 2007 and was followed by a second wave in 2016 (Aldaghishy, 2019, pp. 85–91). Alongside the public schools, all countries in the region have significant enrolments in private schools. In Lebanon, the proportion reached 66% in 2013/14 (Abouchedid & Bou Zeid, 2017, p. 70), reflecting not only the demands of diverse religious, cultural and political groups but also neoliberal forces that had contributed to closure of public schools (Mahfouz, 2021, p. 112). Yet although these parents were paying fees to private schools, many paid additional fees for private tutoring (Al-Haj, 2018).

In the school sector, the marketisation initiatives were consistent with advice in an influential World Bank report entitled *The Road Not Traveled: Education Reform in the Middle East and North Africa*. Its main finding (World Bank, 2008, pp. 2–3) was that the region had made significant strides in the education sector, having started in the 1960s and 1970s from very low levels of human capital accumulation, but had not capitalised fully on investments or developed education systems capable of meeting new challenges. Thus, the report (p. xv) emphasised the central role of incentives to meet sector goals:

> Most reforms in the region have attempted to *engineer* changes in the education system: building schools, hiring teachers, and writing curricula. The success of future reforms will require instead changes in the *behavior* of key education actors – teachers, administrators, and educational authorities. This is the road not traveled in the education sector.

The report also recommended encouragement of voices from civil society in order increase the accountability of government personnel.

Nevertheless, the emphases in the Qatari and Saudi reforms and in the World Bank document had certain ironies. While the advocates recommended introduction of market elements to improve accountability and incentives, reflecting neoclassical ideology, they did not have in mind private tutoring as an expression of that orientation. And while they recommended encouragement of voices from civil society, they did not have in mind the de facto expression of agency through parental demand for tutoring. The World Bank report did have a few references to tutoring, most notably in a box about the phenomenon in Egypt (World Bank, 2008, p. 190). However, these references were generally tangential, and private tutoring was not addressed with the same sorts of rigour as private schooling. Somehow the virtues of privatisation as espoused in these documents were attached only to schooling rather than to its shadow. Indeed, if tutoring was addressed at all, it was with a negative label (e.g. World Bank, 2008, p. 189).

Returning to questions of commonality and difference, instructive patterns may be noted in the identities of tutoring providers. Overall, it seems that by far the dominant providers in the 12 countries addressed here are serving teachers, small tutoring centres and other informal workers. The wealth of the GCC countries has attracted multinational operators, such as Kumon, Oxford Learning, Kip McGrath and Sylvan Learning, but they are only a minor presence.[1] Further, although Box 4.2 presented a major Saudi company working across national borders and harnessing technology, large companies for face-to-face tutoring of the types found in Hong Kong and Korea (Eng, 2019; Kim & Park, 2013), which in many cases are quoted on national or even international stock exchanges, are not widely evident.[2]

A further matter deserving more research concerns the roles of university students. In the UAE, 78% of the parents responding to the survey administered by Rocha and Hamed (2018, p. 28) stated that they would not hire college undergraduates because, in the researchers' interpretation, 'those tutors would probably be young and have limited experience in teaching'. That fact is in striking contrast to patterns in Denmark, for example. In that country, the leading tutoring company bases its entire operation on undergraduates as tutors precisely because they are young and thus are seen as more accessible role models especially for teenagers (Christensen et al., 2021; Kany, 2021). Thus in this respect cultural factors again come into play, particularly when also much tutoring is conducted in the tutees' homes, and therefore in the Middle East gender factors must be considered carefully.

Finding balances

Much discourse about private tutoring by officials, academics and journalists is very negative. For example:

- In *Iraq*, a journalist (Almada Paper, 2015) described private tutoring as a 'cancer [that] has spread in the body of education'; and Raoof and Hamo (2017, p. 253), writing as academics, similarly described tutoring as 'a dangerous phenomenon that can lead to the collapse of the educational system'.
- In *Kuwait*, Al-Sowelan (2013, p. 13), writing as an academic, declared that for educators 'the phenomenon of private tutoring has become a disease . . . [needing] different ways to treat it, search for its causes and limit its spread'. Likewise, a group of researchers for the Ministry of Education stressed 'the dangers of private tutoring and its negative impact' (Al-Mekrabi et al., 2011, p. 4). They were echoed by subsequent researchers for the Ministry who described tutoring as 'a major threat to the educational system' and who had 'the aim of limiting its spread and eliminating it' (Mahmoud & Al-Dhafiri, 2021, p. 1).
- In *Palestine*, the Director of Legal Service attached to the Ministry of Education is reported to have described private tutoring as 'creating a lot of trouble to the educational process by wasting the time and money of the students and the effort of mainstream teachers' (Paltoday, 2010).

- In *Qatar*, the President of the Bar Association (quoted by Mukhtar, 2015) focused on the newspaper advertisements for tutoring, mostly offered by non-nationals. 'No one knows how these people enter', he said, asserting that the majority did not have appropriate visas. He added that they were 'exhausting families with the costs of lessons; [that] nobody limits these fraudsters, and [that] their situation is like that of intruders . . . who work in secret'. A colleague in the Bar Association described private tutoring as 'a profession for those who do not have a profession'.
- In the *UAE*, Khaled Al-Marri (quoted by Al-Mahi, 2021), writing as an educational expert, highlighted the financial burden of private tutoring on families and 'the additional burden on students due to their preoccupation with tutoring that consumes a lot of time and leaves them mentally and physically exhausted'. Tutoring, he added, 'also causes students' laziness and permanent dependence on an external source for study', and leads to neglect of schooling because students know that they have another source of information. Al-Marri added that private tutoring had 'become more dangerous after its spread through distance education, as it allows anyone to claim educational experience and practice the profession'.

Yet other commentators (e.g. Al Farra, 2009; Al-Jaffal, 2017; Alotaibi, 2014; Jiffry, 2012) are more balanced. They recognise that tutoring assists with learning and development of human capital, and that it can complement school-based learning by helping slow learners to keep up with their peers and by stretching high achievers to greater heights. They add that tutoring provides jobs in tutorial centres and self-employment for informal workers. It also supplements the salaries of teachers, thereby allowing governments and operators of private schools (justifiably or unjustifiably) to pay relatively low salaries but nevertheless keep the teachers in the profession. Private tutoring is also attractive to parents because their children are perceived to do better in school, and are gainfully occupied under supervision outside school hours.

Further, under certain circumstances private tutoring can even strengthen school systems. Because tutors are less constrained by traditions and bureaucracies, they may embark on innovations, for example in design of learning aids and use of technology, that in the longer run benefit the schools. Even teachers who provide supplementary tutoring may have enhanced rather than diminished school performance. As noted by Wattar (2014, p. 177), when the Syrian education authorities sought to reduce memorisation and fact-based approaches in favour of more communicative and task-based learning, some teachers who were providing tutoring felt threatened but others seized the innovation and managed it well in schools in order to 'keep their name' in the marketplace. Further, private tutoring allowed teachers to reclaim their professional autonomy as they sought ways to be creative beyond the constraints of school-supervised processes (Wattar, 2014, p. 62).

Yet whatever these negative and positive dimensions, tutoring has certainly become a norm in the Middle East for families across income groups. Thus, it is especially evident among the middle classes and to some extent the upper classes (though they have alternative routes to maintain their social positions), and is even evident for many in the lower classes because they feel that without tutoring they have no chance of competition. Writing about Qatar but with wider relevance, Stepney (2016, p. 4) observed that high enrolment rates in tutoring were sustained by normalisation: 'the perceived advantage conferred by extra tutoring carries a desirability effect that encourages more parents and students to use tutors, regardless of strict academic need'. Yet tutoring is certainly a great financial burden for lower-class families; and many in the lowest income groups are left out entirely and thus in effect lose the competition at the starting line. As such, private tutoring raises major issues of social stratification.

The question then arises what policy makers, particularly in central government but also at subnational levels, can and should do about the phenomenon. The answer must to a large extent depend on economic and political circumstances. A strong case can be made for regulation both of teachers who desire to offer supplementary tutoring and of commercial enterprises, though informal suppliers such as university students and retirees are more difficult to regulate. Yet the extent to which regulations of teachers and enterprises can be made to work depends on the attitudes and motivations of actors in the educational ecosystems, which are themselves at least partly shaped by resourcing.

Elaborating, a regulatory priority would be to prohibit teachers from tutoring their existing students. This measure would avoid temptations by the teachers deliberately to underperform in regular lessons in order to promote their private classes. It would also avoid the corruption noted by the Saudi parent when her son's tutor indicated that for an extra 2,000 riyals he would provide in advance the questions for the final examination and help her son with the answers (see Chapter 5).

Whether regulations should then move to prohibition of all private tutoring by serving teachers is a matter for careful consideration in the light of balances and capacity to enforce. Precedents in Korea and China show that under some circumstances it is possible to change engrained cultures, even if the process requires swimming against the tide, and to stop serving teachers from providing supplementary tutoring (Bray, 2021c; Zhang, 2019;

Kim, 2016). The measure requires strong financing, in particular, paying teachers adequately in order to remove the justification that they need supplementary incomes for basic family needs, and it requires strong government with both tenacity and ability to follow through with implementation. It is aided by public consensus about the desirability for such a policy, so that parents will be less likely to ask teachers for such support and teachers will be more likely to decline if they are asked.

Beyond that basic starting point, some differentiation seems necessary among the Middle East countries. The GCC countries have the economic resources to follow the Korean and Chinese paths, together with administrative machinery at least with the public schools that they control directly. Private schools may require further consideration in the light of legal frameworks and traditions of autonomy; but possibilities certainly exist for negotiation with the private sector. The lower-income countries face greater challenges because the authorities cannot so easily remove the economic justification for teachers providing supplementary tutoring. In these settings, persuasion may be needed as much as direct instruction.

For such persuasion, a good place to start is with the media for general publicity and then with the schools themselves. In contrast to anonymous statistics and broadly phrased circulars, at the school level the teachers, students and parents are known people with personal faces. Much then depends on the perspectives of the school leadership and the ways in which they manage circumstances. This observation applies not only to public schools but also to private ones. Box 7.1 presents the strategy adopted by one private school in Dubai.[3] Again, governments would be wise to recognise diversity when engaging in dialogue. Among the instructive features of the case in Box 7.1 is divergence of perspectives even between the primary and secondary sections of the same school. Nevertheless, government presentation of issues to the school level can encourage administrations to think through issues and to discuss not only with teachers but also with parents. The parental perspectives are crucial, though commonly neglected, since the parents are paying for the tutoring and are the vehicle for demand.

The next question concerns regulation of tutorial centres. Referring again to Korea and China, a further factor underpinning the success in those countries in eliminating tutoring by serving teachers has been the existence of a strong private sector of tutorial centres. These centres, it must be admitted, have served some populations better than others. They have mainly been located in urban areas, with concentrations in districts that have large numbers of families in the target income groups. Nevertheless, technologies now permit distance education so that even rural families can access many services from such companies. Again these circumstances can more easily be replicated in the high-income GCC countries than in the lower-income

Box 7.1 A School-Driven Approach to Private Tutoring in Dubai

Schools in Dubai have had widely different attitudes towards private tutoring, and attitudes may differ between even the primary and secondary sections of the same school. The following portrait is of an English-medium school following a UK curriculum in which leadership of the primary section decided to bring tutoring into the school rather than leave it outside.

In order to manage this process, the school appointed a co-ordinator of learning support to organise extra fee-paying lessons for students according to demand. She only works with the primary section. The secondary section differs because the leadership is strongly opposed to tutoring and will not permit it. Attitudes and expectations in the primary section differ in part because of the ambitions of the leadership. Students are described as being 1½ years ahead of the national curriculum, though ironically at the end of primary 40% of students go to other schools in Dubai. The secondary section thus has lower standards. It takes students from elsewhere, and the lower achievers from primary.

The co-ordinator of learning support organises extra tutoring by teachers in the school. Parents are charged 250 dirhams (US$68) per hour, of which 25 dirhams are taken by the school and 225 dirhams are remitted to the teacher. This is done officially, through the finance office. For most students the support is remedial, but provision also exists for enrichment. Teachers are not permitted to tutor their own students, but it is considered important that the tutors are indeed teachers from this school since they know the curriculum and the mechanics and traditions. All tutoring is one-to-one, and about half of the teachers provide tutoring through the school's arrangement.

Part way through the spoken presentation of this arrangement, one of the tutors joined in. When asked about the attitude of teachers, including whether they ease up because they know that the students can be tutored, she remarked that the teachers do seem more relaxed than their UK counterparts. In the UK, she said, teachers would have to take responsibility for the students' grades, and would not be permitted to fail to get the students up to the mark.

Evaluation of tutoring is done by the parents, but the co-ordinator of learning support is also doing some tracking. The parents know who are the really good teachers, and ask for those. The parents discuss

> with other parents. Some teachers are pressurised by parents to offer tutoring, but not all agree. Those who do agree have the classes after the end of the day, always on campus. Many also give tutoring on Saturdays.
> Some teachers resent the school taking the 25 dirhams levy. Indeed, some teachers are willing to tutor for even less than 225 dirhams just to prevent the school receiving the levy. But the co-ordinator of learning support feels that the school really deserves the levy because she devotes much labour. She is also doing some quality control – getting the tutors to prepare lesson plans and be more transparent and systematic.

countries of the Middle East, but they should still be borne in mind by policy makers. Thus, a strong private sector can in some respects support the public education system and remove the argument that teachers should provide private supplementary tutoring because families have no alternatives.

The aforementioned remarks, and this book as a whole, show that the issues surrounding private supplementary tutoring are complex. When devising appropriate responses, and proactively thinking ahead to a desirable vision, policy makers in the Middle East can learn a lot not only from their immediate neighbours but also from countries in more distant locations and cultures. The corollary is that counterparts elsewhere can learn a lot from patterns in the Middle East. This book has drawn on much Arabic-language literature that has not been easily accessible to readers in other world regions, and part of the global contribution of the book is to make the experiences known to readers through the medium of English.

Among the lessons from this analysis and from international comparisons is that private tutoring, whether in the form of shadow mimicry or in extension beyond mainstream school curricula, will not simply go away. In the countries addressed by this book, private tutoring has been a significant issue even since the 1960s (Jamal, 1965) and expanding during the 1970s and 1980s (Al-Khatib, 1982; Hussein, 1987; Junaidi, 1977); and elsewhere in the region – especially Egypt – the concern has an even longer history with regulations dating from the 1940s (Egypt, 1947). With the growing power of neoliberalism in the education sector alongside other domains (Abdel-Moneim, 2016; Arar et al., 2021; Chitpin & Portelli, 2019; Verger et al., 2016), state-run education systems are increasingly shaped by market forces, whether by design or by default. The present authors would not go so far as recommending a government-run voucher system for families to access private tutoring, as was envisaged by Rocha and Hamed (2018, p. 31), since that would require far-reaching quality-control measures for governments to decide what sorts of tutoring they would legitimise and what sorts they would avoid; but certainly policy makers need to catch up with a reality that has long been known by most families in the Middle East and is increasingly known even in Scandinavia and elsewhere, namely that schooling can satisfy the bulk of educational needs but that other channels and inputs are also available and useful.

The final summary of the present work, therefore, is that private tutoring will be an enduring phenomenon but will also evolve. Much of the evolution will be driven by forces beyond the control of policy makers in Ministries of Education and schools. These forces include economics, politics, technological advance and expanded interconnectedness through globalisation. Some aspects of private supplementary tutoring may be welcomed, while others may have to be tolerated. At the same time, policy makers do have ways to steer the sector. Those in well-resourced countries have more instruments available for such steering, but even in the less-resourced countries, much can be achieved through public discussion and consensus-building. Thus, overall the greatest need is to take the topic out of the shadows, with stronger research-based data and with analysis that takes account of the motives and consequent actions of all stakeholders in the education ecosystem.

Notes

1 In 2021, these four companies between them operated only 22 centres in the six GCC countries (and none in the six other countries considered here).
2 Such companies also emerged in China during the 2010s (see Feng, 2021), though were later abruptly curtailed by national regulations (China, 2021).
3 Box 7.1 is based on notes taken by Mark Bray during a visit to learn about school perspectives on private tutoring. The date of the visit has been omitted to help protect anonymity.

References

Abdel-Moneim, Mohamed Alaa (2016): *A Political Economy of Arab Education: Policies and Comparative Perspectives*. London: Routledge.

Abdel-Moneim, Mohamed Alaa (2020): 'Between Global and National Prescriptions for Educational Administration: The Rocky Road of Neoliberal Education Reform in Qatar'. *International Journal of Educational Development*, Vol.74, pp. 1–16.

Abouchedid, Kamal & Bou Zeid, Maria (2017): 'Lebanon: Legacy of the Past and Present Challenges', in Kirdar, Serra (ed.), *Education in the Arab World*. London: Bloomsbury, pp. 59–84.

Aldaghishy, Thamir (2019): *The Influence of the Global Education Reform Movement on Saudi Arabia's Education Policy Reforms: A Qualitative Study*. PhD dissertation, St Louis University.

Al Farra, Samia (2009): *Private Tuition Phenomenon in Mathematics in Greater Amman – Jordan: Does Private Tuition Improve Achievement in Mathematics?*. Saarbrücken: VDM Verlag Dr. Müller.

Al-Haj, Faten (2018): 'Private Tutoring Institutes: A Censorship-Free Business – Lebanese are Paying for Two Schools'. *Al-Akhbar*, 1 April. https://al-akhbar.com/Education/247538 [in Arabic]

Al-Khatib, Ahmed (1982): *The Phenomenon of Private Tutoring Received by Secondary School Students in Jordan*. Amman: Ministry of Education, Directorate of Planning & Educational Research. ظاهرة الدروس الخصوصية عند طلبة الصف الثالث الثانوي في المدارس الأردنية [in Arabic]

Al-Jaffal, Omar (2017): 'The Majority of Iraqi Students Depend on Private Tutoring'. *Ultrasawt*, 18 March. الدروس الخصوصية في العراق مدارس موازية [in Arabic]

Almada Paper (2015): 'Private Tutoring Is a Market for Supply and Demand', 16 August. الدروس الخصوصية سوق للعرض والطلب [in Arabic]

Al-Mahi, Muhammed (2021): 'Private Tutoring Is a Parental Strategy to Compensate for the Poor Follow-up'. *Alkhaleej Newspaper*, 5 June. الدروس الخصوصية وسيلة أسر لتعويض "تقصير" المتابعة [in Arabic]

Al-Mekrabi, Mohammed Abdul Rahim; Afifi, Mohammed Abbas; Abdullah, Hessein; Warak, Safaa & Alenzi, Aisha (2011): *The Phenomenon of Private Tutoring [in Kuwait]: Causes and Solutions (Unpublished Report)*, Kuwait City: Ministry of Education [in Arabic].

Alotaibi, Ghazi N. (2014): 'Causes of Private Tutoring in English: Perspectives of Saudi Secondary School Students and Their Parents'. *Studies in Literature and Language*, Vol. 8, No. 3, pp. 79–83.

Al-Sowelan, Zoha'a F. (2013): 'Factors Related to the Spread of Private Tutoring in the Secondary School Unified System in Kuwait'. *The Education Journal*, Vol.27, No.107, pp. 13–52. عوامل انتشار ظاهرة الدروس الخصوصية بدولة الكويت [in Arabic]

Arar, Khalid; Örücü, Deniz & Wilkinson, Jane (eds.) (2021): *Neoliberalism and Education Systems in Conflict: Exploring Challenges across the Globe*. London: Routledge.

Bíró, Zsuzsanna Hanna (2020). Az árnyékoktatásról internetes magánoktatói hirdetések tükrében [On Shadow Education in the Light of Online Private Tutor Ads]. *Educatio*, 29(2), 243–260. [in Hungarian]

Bray, Mark (2021c): 'Swimming Against the Tide: Comparative Lessons From Government Efforts to Prohibit Private Supplementary Tutoring Delivered by Regular Teachers'. *Hungarian Educational Research Journal*, Vol.11, No.2, pp. 168–188.

Bray, Mark & Ventura, Alexandre (2022): Multiple Systems, Multiple Shadows: Diversity of Supplementary Tutoring Received by Private-School Students in Dubai. *International Journal of Educational Development*, Vol.92, pp. 1–8.

Brewer, Dominic J. & Goldman, Charles A. (2010): 'An Introduction to Qatar's Primary and Secondary Education Reform', in Abi-Mershed, Osama (ed.), *Trajectories of Education in the Arab World: Legacies and Challenges*. New York: Routledge, pp. 226–246.

China, CPC [Communist Party of China] Central Committee and the General Office of the State Council (2021): *Policy on Further Reducing the Workload of Students and the Burden of Out-of-School Training in the Compulsory Education Stage*. Beijing: Ministry of Education. [in Chinese] https://mp.weixin.qq.com/s/-Qd8YcNaEx_3Y2qkTe3WOA

Chitpin, Stephanie & Portelli, John P. (eds.) (2019): *Confronting Educational Policy in Neoliberal Times: International Perspectives*. New York: Routledge.

Christensen, Søren; Grønbek & Bækdahl, Frederik (2021): 'The Private Tutoring Industry in Denmark: Market Making and Modes of Moral Justification'. *ECNU Review of Education* [East China Normal University], Vol.4, No.3, pp. 520–545. https://journals.sagepub.com/doi/pdf/10.1177/2096531120960742

El-Emadi, Ahmad A.; Said, Ziad; & Friesen, Heather L. (2019): 'Teaching Style Differences between Male and Female Science Teachers in Qatari Schools: Possible Impact on Student Achievement'. *EURASIA Journal of Mathematics, Science and Technology Education*, Vol.15, No.12, pp. 1–16.

Egypt, Ministry of Education (1947): 'The Organisation of Private [Supplementary] Lessons for Students'. Ministerial Circular No.7530. Cairo: Ministry of Education. [in Arabic]

Eng, Richard (2019): 'The Tutoring Industry in Hong Kong: From the Past Four Decades to the Future'. *ECNU Review of Education* [East China Normal University], Vol.2, No.1, pp. 77–86. https://journals.sagepub.com/doi/full/10.1177/2096531119840857

Feng, Siyuan (2021): 'The Evolution of Shadow Education in China: From Emergence to Capitalisation'. *Hungarian Educational Research Journal*, Vol.11, No.2, pp. 89–100.

Hussein, Mansour G. A. (1987): 'Private Tutoring: A Hidden Educational Problem'. *Educational Studies in Mathematics*, Vol.18, No.1, pp. 91–96.

Jamal, Ahmed Mohamed (1965): 'Perspectives and Reflections on Education and Sociology'. *Journal of Hajj and Umrah* [Saudi Arabia], Vol.8, pp. 483–484. نظرات وتأملات في محيط التربية والتعليم والاجتماع [in Arabic]

Jiffry, Fadia (2012): 'Private Tuition Becoming an Increasing Trend among Teachers'. *Arab News*, 29 November. www.arabnews.com/private-tuition-becoming-increasing-trend-among-teachers-0

Junaidi, Salah (1977): 'Empirical Study of Private Tutoring in Saudi Arabia', summarised in Saudi Arabia, Ministry of Education (1978): 'Introducing some Educational Documents'. *Journal of Educational Documentation*, Vol.15, pp. 86–104. تعريف بوثائق تربوية [in Arabic]

Kany, Nicklas (2021): 'The Rise of Private Tutoring in Denmark: An Entrepreneur's Perspectives and Experiences'. *ECNU Review of Education* [East China Normal University], Vol.4, No.3, pp. 630–639. https://journals.sagepub.com/doi/full/10.1177/20965311211038560

Kim, Kyung-Min & Park, Daekwon (2013): 'Impacts of Urban Economic Factors on Private Tutoring Industry'. *Asia Pacific Education Review*, Vol.13, No.2, pp. 273–280.

Kim, Young-Chun (2016): *Shadow Education and the Curriculum and Culture of Schooling in South Korea*. New York: Palgrave Macmillan.

Mahfouz, Julia (2021): 'Neoliberalism – The Straw that Broke the Back of Lebanon's Education System', in Arar, Khalid; Örücü, Deniz & Wilkinson, Jane (eds.), *Neoliberalism and Education Systems in Conflict: Exploring Challenges Across the Globe*. London: Routledge, pp. 107–117.

Mahmoud, Ashraf Arabi Khalil & Al-Dhafiri, Iman Muhammed Jadee (2021): *Report about the Phenomenon of Private Tutoring and Ways to Limit its Spread in the State of Kuwait*. Kuwait: Educational Research and Curriculum Sector, Ministry of Education.

Mukhtar, Mahmoud (2015): 'The Punishment of Private Tutoring Dealers Is to Be Prison'. *Alarab*, 6 October. السجن ينتظر تجار الدروس الخصوصية [in Arabic]

Paltoday (2010): 'The Ministry of Education decided to ban private tutoring and warned to prosecute and sue the offenders'. *Paltoday*, 2 September. وزارة التعليم تقرر منع الدروس الخصوصية وتحذر المخالفين [in Arabic].

Qatar, Ministry of Education and Higher Education (2020): *Annual Statistics of Education in the State of Qatar 2017–2018*. Doha: Ministry of Education and Higher Education.

Raoof, Tamara & Hamo, Khlood Yousef (2017): 'The Spread of Tutoring in Iraq's Institutions: Causes and Factors'. *Journal of Kirkuk University for Administrative and Economic Sciences*, Vol.7, No.1, pp. 252–270. انتشار ظاهرة التعليم الخصوصي في مؤسسات العراق: الأسباب والعوامل [in Arabic]

Rocha, Valeria & Hamed, Sheren (2018): *Parents' Perspectives on Paid Private Tutoring in the United Arab Emirates*. Sharjah: UNESCO Regional Center for Educational Planning.

Stepney, Erin (2016): *Shadow Education: Private Tutoring and Education Reform*. Doha: Social & Economic Survey Research Institute (SESRI), Qatar University.

Verger, Antoni; Fontdevila, Clara & Zancajo, Adrián (2016): *The Privatization of Education: A Political Economy of Global Education Reform*. New York: Teachers College Press.

Wattar, Dania (2014): *Globalization, Curriculum Reform and Teacher Professional Development in Syria*. PhD thesis, University of Alberta.

World Bank, The (2008): *The Road Not Traveled: Education Reform in the Middle East and North Africa*. Washington: The World Bank. https://openknowledge.worldbank.org/bitstream/handle/10986/6303/467890PUB0Box31DU1Flagship1Full1ENG.pdf?sequence=1&isAllowed=y

Zhang, Wei (2019): 'Regulating Private Tutoring in China: Uniform Policies, Diverse Responses'. *ECNU Review of Education* [East China Normal University], Vol.2, No.1, pp. 25–43. https://journals.sagepub.com/doi/full/10.1177/2096531119840868

Notes on the Authors

Mark Bray is a distinguished chair professor and director of the Centre for International Research in Supplementary Tutoring (CIRIST) in the Faculty of Education at East China Normal University, Shanghai. He is also Emeritus Professor holding the UNESCO Chair in Comparative Education at the University of Hong Kong.

Professor Bray commenced his career as a school teacher in Kenya and then Nigeria, and subsequently taught at the Universities of Edinburgh, Papua New Guinea and London. He joined the University of Hong Kong in 1986. Between 2006 and 2010, he took leave from Hong Kong to work in Paris as director of UNESCO's International Institute for Educational Planning (IIEP). He commenced his work in Shanghai in 2018.

Professor Bray is also a past-president of the Comparative Education Society of Hong Kong (CESHK), the US-based Comparative and International Education Society (CIES), and the World Council of Comparative Education Societies (WCCES). He is known for his pioneering research on the theme of shadow education across the world and including parts of the Middle East. Among his books on shadow education are translations into 23 languages, including Arabic.

Anas Hajar is a graduate of Warwick University in England, holding a PhD in language education. He commenced his career as a teacher in primary and secondary schools and as an English-language lecturer at Aleppo University, Syria. He has also worked as a post-doctoral research and teaching fellow at Warwick, Coventry and Christ Church Universities in England, and at the Chinese University of Hong Kong.

Dr Hajar is currently an associate professor of multilingual education, and the PhD programme director, in the Faculty of Education at Nazarbayev University, Kazakhstan. He is particularly interested in motivational issues in language learning and in intercultural engagement. He also works in the areas of shadow education, internationalisation, education abroad and language learning strategies.

Index

Abdel-Moneim, M. A. 18, 22, 24, 47, 84, 86, 93–94
academic achievement xvii, xviii, 16, 22, 36, 43, 47–48, 55–56, 58–59, 70
advertise/advertisement 6, 9, 39, 44, 52, 72–73, 76, 78, 89
Aldaghishy, T. 21, 24, 43, 48, 64, 71, 77, 86, 95
Arab countries xxi, 8, 50, 79
Arabic 1–2, 16–18, 23–24, 28–29, 31, 36–37, 83–84, 93, 98
Arab World 24–25, 49–52, 94, 96

backwash xxi, 57
Bahrain 2, 17–18, 20, 24, 27–28, 30, 32–34, 39, 47–48, 59, 61, 63, 71
Bray, M. xx–xxii, 1–5, 7, 9–12, 15, 20, 39, 42, 48–50, 69, 73, 75–77, 79, 84, 90, 94–95
bureaucracy/bureaucratic 34, 46, 89

China 7, 11, 90–91, 94, 96–97
Christensen, S. 7, 12, 70, 79, 88, 96
competition/competitive/competing xvii, xix, 10, 36, 43, 69, 73, 83, 90
corruption 12, 58, 74, 90
cost 21, 33, 47, 49, 72–73, 82, 89
Covid-19 5, 33, 35, 52, 69
curriculum/curricula xix, 4, 11, 13–16, 22, 26, 30, 34, 38–39, 41, 43, 51, 55, 63–64, 69–72, 79–80, 82, 85–87, 92–93, 97

dependence 55, 57, 59, 89
distance education/distance learning 47, 89, 91
Dubai 19–22, 24–26, 30–32, 38, 46–47, 50–51, 56, 58–60, 73, 75, 79, 84, 91–92, 95

East Asia 1, 3, 7–8, 13–14, 19
East China Normal University (ECNU) 3, 12, 79, 96–97
economic xvi, xvii, xxi, 17–18, 21–23, 28, 31, 36, 42, 83–84, 90–91, 94
education system xxi, 2, 10–12, 17, 22–23, 25, 31, 45, 70, 84, 86–87, 93, 95, 97
Egypt xvii, 8, 10–13, 15, 18–19, 30, 35, 42, 47, 61, 71, 76, 84, 87, 93, 96
enrichment 21, 65, 74, 92
Entrich, S. 1, 3, 10, 13, 30, 36, 50
examination period/examination season 36, 40
expatriate 19, 29–30, 45, 63

family(ies) 15, 17, 19, 23–24, 29, 33–34, 36–38, 42–49, 51, 55, 59, 63, 67, 69, 70–71, 73, 78, 83–84, 86, 89–91, 93–94
favouritism 57
fee-free education 25, 59
fee-free tutoring xvi, 46
financial burden 13, 48, 60, 77

gender 16, 39–40, 52, 59, 68, 85–86, 88
geography/geographic xviii, 6, 13, 37, 42, 47, 49

Germany 11, 22, 38, 85
government schools 16, 30, 38–39, 55, 64–65
group tutoring 9, 33, 47
Gulf Cooperation Council (GCC) xvi, xxi, 1, 18–20, 22, 24, 26, 45–47, 70, 72, 83–85, 87, 91, 94

Hamed, S. xxii, 31, 33–34, 40, 47, 52, 56–57, 61, 74, 81, 88, 94, 97
high-stakes examinations xix, 29, 32, 36, 53, 70, 78

income xvi, xvii, xix, 5, 8–10, 17–18, 21–22, 29, 31, 33–34, 39, 42, 44–46, 66, 71, 73, 83–84, 90–91
India xvii, 6–8, 12–14, 19, 22, 30, 38–39, 42, 64, 73, 83–85
internet 33, 35, 42, 44, 54
Iraq xvi, 1–2, 17–19, 23–24, 27–28, 38–39, 44, 51–52, 63, 66–68, 71, 76, 79, 81–82, 84, 88, 95, 97
Islam/Islamic 16, 22–23, 85

Japan 6–7, 10, 13–14, 22, 38, 83, 85
Jordan xvi, 1–2, 17–18, 24, 27–28, 30, 32–34, 38–39, 44, 47–49, 55, 58, 60, 62–63, 65–66, 70–71, 77, 79, 84–85, 95

Knowledge & Human Development Authority (KHDA) 21–22, 25–26, 30, 38, 51, 56, 60, 73, 76
Korea, Republic of 7, 9, 14–15, 61, 70, 79, 88, 90–91, 97
Kuwait xvi, 1–2, 8, 17–18, 20, 24–25, 27, 29, 31–34, 38, 47–51, 59–60, 63, 66, 70–73, 75, 77–80, 82, 88, 95, 97

laissez faire xix, 22, 62, 69
large classes 6, 38, 54, 71
large-class tutoring 33, 54
League of Arab States 39, 48, 51
Lebanon xvi, 1, 17–19, 22, 24–27, 29, 32–35, 50, 62, 68–69, 84, 86, 94, 97
licence/license 21, 43, 63–64, 67–69, 72, 82

market/marketplace xvii, xxii, 3, 5, 8, 10, 14–16, 21, 28, 42–43, 47, 63, 66, 78, 86–87, 90, 93, 95–96
media xix, 2, 63, 67, 75, 91
Middle East xvi, xvii, xxi, 1–3, 16, 25, 72, 83, 87, 90, 93–94
Middle East and North Africa (MENA) 1, 18, 52, 70, 84
Middle East countries xvi, 8, 17, 28, 63, 68, 74, 86, 91
Middle East cultures 39, 60
Middle East region xxi, 27
modes (of private tutoring) 5–6, 33, 43, 54, 70

Oman xvi, 1–2, 17–18, 20, 24–25, 27, 29, 32, 34, 39, 48, 51, 59–60, 64, 66, 72–73, 78, 80
one-to-one/one-to-one tutoring 4–5, 9, 33–34, 54, 59, 64–65, 76, 92
online 4–6, 31, 33–34, 52, 95

Palestine xvi, xvii, 1, 17, 19, 24, 29–30, 39, 59, 64, 66, 70–71, 84, 88
partnership xix, 72, 74–75
peers 9–10, 36, 38, 54, 57, 74, 89
penalty 64, 67–68
performance xvii, 21, 36–38, 45, 56–57, 60–61, 66, 70, 72, 89
policy forum 2, 47
policy implications xxii, 1, 3, 12, 24, 62
policy makers xviii, xix, xxi, xxii, 1, 66, 70, 74–75, 90, 93–94
political diversities 17
political forces xxi, 2, 22
primary education/primary level xvi, 5, 14, 27–28, 31, 50, 69, 76
private schools 20, 22–23, 28, 38–39, 41, 64, 73, 84, 86–87, 89, 91–92, 96
Programme for International Student Assessment (PISA) 22, 30
prohibition xix, 45, 65–66, 73, 90
providers xix, 5–6, 87
provision xix, 4–5, 18, 39, 44, 52, 62–63, 72, 92

Index

Qatar xvi, xvii, xix, 8, 17–20, 22, 24–25, 30, 32–34, 36, 40, 43–45, 47–48, 50, 52, 57, 64–65, 68, 72, 81, 84–86, 89, 90, 97

Regional Center for Educational Planning (RCEP) xxi, 1–2, 47, 76
regulations xviii, xix, xxi, 8, 11, 21, 26, 38, 62–69, 72–73, 90, 93–94
remedial lessons/remedial support 21, 63, 75, 78, 80, 92
Ridge, N. 19, 26, 44, 47, 52
Rocha, V. xxii, 31, 33–34, 40, 47, 52, 56–57, 61, 74, 81, 88, 94, 97

salary(ies) xvii, xix, 8–10, 25, 28–30, 33, 42, 44–45, 49, 65, 67, 70, 73, 89
Saudi Arabia xvi, xvii, 1, 17, 20–22, 24–27, 30, 33–35, 42, 44–45, 47–48, 50–51, 62, 64–66, 71, 76–77, 79, 81, 86, 95–96
scale xvi, 1–3, 9, 19, 24, 27–28, 65, 76, 84
scores xvii, 35–36, 55
secondary education/schooling xvi, xvii, 5–7, 27–32, 49–50, 70, 76, 96
Sellami, A. 30, 36, 38, 40, 48, 52, 64, 81, 86
serving teachers xix, 10, 62–63, 66, 73, 87, 90–91
Silova, I. xxii, 1, 3, 5, 15, 73, 81
small-group/small groups 4–6, 33–34, 38–39, 47, 54, 87
social inequalities xviii, 13, 20

social values xviii, 58
supply xvii, xix, 8, 10–11, 42, 44, 74, 95
Syria xvi, xvii, 1–2, 17–19, 23–26, 30, 42, 44, 49, 57, 64, 66–68, 71–73, 76–78, 80–82, 84–85, 89, 97

technology(ies) xviii, 5, 33, 35, 71, 88–89, 91, 94
textbooks 4, 26, 71
Trends in International Mathematics and Science Study (TIMSS) xvi, 21, 24, 28–32, 34, 36, 46, 51
tutorial centres xviii, xix, 5, 9, 43, 62, 67–69, 72–73, 89, 91
tutorial enterprises 42, 44
tutorial institutes 64, 67

UNESCO xxi, xxii, 1
UNICEF 71, 76, 82
United Arab Emirates (UAE) xvi, 1, 2, 18–21, 24, 27, 30, 32–34, 38, 40–41, 44, 47, 50, 52, 56–57, 61–62, 66, 69, 73–74, 77, 79, 81, 84, 88–89
United Nations 20, 26, 39, 67

World Bank 26, 79, 87, 97

Yemen xvi, xvii, 1–2, 17–19, 23–26, 31, 42, 44, 49, 51, 62, 70, 75–76, 78

Zhang, W. 1, 3, 7, 12, 15, 70, 79, 90, 97

For Product Safety Concerns and Information please contact our EU representative GPSR@taylorandfrancis.com
Taylor & Francis Verlag GmbH, Kaufingerstraße 24, 80331 München, Germany

www.ingramcontent.com/pod-product-compliance
Lightning Source LLC
Chambersburg PA
CBHW070557170426
43201CB00012B/1863